Colin F. Taylor, Ph. D.

Sun'ka Wakan
Sacred Horses of the Plains Indians: Ethos and Regalia

Heilige Pferde der Plainsindianer: Ethos und Regalia

Colin F. Taylor, Ph. D.

Sun'ka Wakan

Sacred Horses of the Plains Indians:
Ethos and Regalia

Heilige Pferde der Plainsindianer:
Ethos und Regalia

Verlag fuer Amerikanistik
Wyk auf Foehr
Germany

Lecture given to the "Plains Indian Art Symposium", Cody, Wyoming, September 1994, checked and enhanced by the author for this book edition.

Illustrations: Colin F. Taylor

German translation: Dietmar Kuegler and Helga M. Kuegler

Cover: Double horse "shield" and associated woman's saddle, ca. 1846. Spalding Park collections, Idaho. Photograph by Bill Holm. See Fig. 62.

ISBN 3-89510-022-6

2. Auflage 1998

Copyright (c) 1995 by VERLAG FUER AMERIKANISTIK, P. O. Box 1332, D-25931 Wyk auf Foehr

Satzherstellung: Druckerei R. Knust GmbH, D-38104 Braunschweig
Druck- und Reproarbeiten: Druckerei R. Knust GmbH, D-38104 Braunschweig
Buchbinderische Verarbeitung: Buchbinderei Bratherig, D-38118 Braunschweig

Alle Rechte der Verbreitung, in jeglicher Form und Technik, vorbehalten!

Printed in Germany

Acknowledgements

This has turned out to be a particularly rewarding research project and it is amazing how much can be reconstructed from the superb studies of Wissler, Bad Heart Bull and later J. C. Ewers, relating to the use of the Plains Indian horse together with resources such as museum specimens and the opinions of knowledgeable individuals.

Hopefully, I have acknowledged all my sources in the text. However, particular thanks go to *Tim Bernadis* (at Crow Agency), *Arni Brownstone, George Horse Capture, Stu Conner, Joe Medicine Crow, Hugh Dempsey, Richard Edwards, J. C. Ewers, Bill Holm, Hans Karkheck, Jonathan King, R. and D. Lessard, Evan Maurer, Dick Pohrt, Paul Ritner, Carson Walks-over-Ice* and *Ian West*, for the willingness to discuss various points which occured in the course of this study.

In particular, *Bill Holm* very generously shared his research notes as well as copies of the late scholar, *Steve Shawleys's* notes on the Spalding horse shield (or „fender") and saddle now at the Nez Perce Historical Park in Spalding, Idaho.

Richard Edwards also kindly provided several illustrations and notes relating to the horse shields and masks and drew my attention to the Miller photograph which shows one of these in use.

Thanks to my publisher, *Dietmar Kuegler*, who encourages the publishing of these papers.

Arni Brownstone, Hugh and James Dempsey made various comments after my Cody talk and these have been taken into consideration in this final version of
SUN'KA WAKAN.

Finally, thanks to *Lillian Turner* and *Peter Hassrick* at the Buffalo Bill Historical Center, Cody, Wyoming, for the many courtesies since I first participated in the Symposiums, more than fifteen years ago.

Finally, thanks to my wife Betty for helping with these projects in so many different ways.

Colin Taylor
January, 1995

Einführung

*Seht sie tänzeln, sie kommen,
wiehernd, sie kommen -
ein Volk von Pferden.*
Two Shields, Teton Sioux. Densmore, 1918

Während die Frage der Verbreitung des Pferdes bei den Plainsindianern, die mythologischen Überlieferungen, die den Ursprung des Pferdes erklären, und die Entwicklung und Art der Pferdeausrüstung der verschiedenen Stämme beachtliche Aufmerksamkeit auf sich gezogen haben (Wissler (1915); Lowie (1922); Haines (1938); Ewers (1955) et al), wurde dem Symbolismus, der mit dem Pferd in der Plainsindianerkultur verbunden ist, insbesondere den verschiedenen Ausrüstungsgegenständen und Verzierungen, die für bestimmte Aussagen in Bezug auf Verpflichtungen, Verdienste, Rang, Status und Machtposition innerhalb der sozialen und religiösen Hierarchie des Stammes stehen, sehr wenig Beachtung geschenkt.

So benutzten beispielsweise die Eigentümer der prestigeträchtigen Blackfeet-Medizinbündel für den Transport des Bündels ein besonders ausgewähltes Pferd; mit diesen Tieren waren bestimmte Tabus verbunden: Sie waren in besonderer Weise bemalt (Abb. 1) und durften - im Fall des Biberbündels - niemals für den Transport von frischem Fleisch benutzt werden.

Außerdem verwendeten Frauen Ausrüstungsgegenstände und Pferdeinsignien, die den Rang, den Reichtum und die militärischen Leistungen ihrer Ehemänner oder Söhne symbolisierten. Derartige Insignien wurden durch den Lakota-Historiker Amos Bad Heart Bull (Blish, 1967), sowie durch den Maler Rudolph Kurz (1937) dargestellt. Eine wunderschöne Schabracke (Abb. 2 und 3), die kürzlich in den europäischen Sammlungen entdeckt wurde, stellte beispielhaft diese Art symbolischer Insignien bezüglich erlittener Wunden, erbeuteter Pferde und verteilter Geschenke dar. (Siehe auch die Abbildungen 15 und 16 im Haupttext.)

Ferner wird der Aspekt des Fransenbesatzes aus Pferdehaar, der ausgiebig an Kriegertrachten benutzt worden war, berücksichtigt werden. Ein beeindruckendes Kleidungsstück, das von dem französischen Entdecker Graf d'Otrante gesammelt wurde und sich jetzt im *Etnografiska Museet* in Stockholm (Schweden) befindet, ist beispielsweise mit Pferdehaarsträhnen verziert, die seinem Blackfeet-Besitzer zufolge (ca. 1849) Pferde repräsentierten, die vom Feind erbeutet wurden; ein ähnlicher Brauch wurde von den Crow berichtet.

Indizien lassen vermuten, daß menschliche Haarsträhnen ebenfalls ein Treuegelöbnis bezeichneten (Moore an Verfasser, 1989), und Pferdehaar schloß die Verpfändung von Pferden ein.

Pferdehaarfransen, häufig grün oder gelb gefärbt, finden sich nicht nur an frühen Sioux-Hemden, wie etwa an jenem, das Francis Parkman 1846 in Fort

Introduction

*See them prancing, they come.
Neighing they come -
a Horse Nation.
Two Shields, Teton Sioux. Densmore, 1918*

While considerable attention has been focussed on the diffusion of the horse to the Plains Indians, the mythological tales which explain its origin and the development and type of horse equipment utilized by various tribes (Wissler (1915); Lowie (1922); Haines (1938); Ewers (1955) et al), very little attention has been given to the symbolism associated with the horse in Plains Indian culture, in particular the various accoutrements and embellishments which made definite statements with regard to obligations, achievements, rank, status and power positions within the social and religious hierarchy of the tribe.

Thus, for example, owners of the prestigious Blackfeet Medicine Bundles used a special horse which was designated for transporting the Bundle and certain taboos were associated with the animals: they were painted a particular way (Fig. 1) and, in the case of the Beaver Bundle, could never be used to transport fresh meat.

Likewise, women used accoutrements and horse regalia which symbolically stated the standing, wealth and military achievements of their husbands or sons. Such regalia was illustrated by the Lakota historian, Amos Bad Heart Bull (Blish, 1967), and also by the artist, Rudolph Kurz (1937). A magnificent caparison (Figs. 2 + 3) recently located in the European collections, exemplifies this type of symbolic regalia, referring to wounds received, horses captured and gifts bestowed. (See also Figs. 15 and 16 in main text).

The aspect of horsehair fringing will also be considered, it being used extensively on warrior costume. For example, an impressive garment collected by the French explorer, Count d'Otrante, and now in the *Etnografiska Museet* in Stockholm, Sweden, is garnished with horsehair locks which according to its Blackfeet owner, circa 1840, were representative of horses captured from the enemy; a similar custom has been described for the Crow.

Circumstantial evidence suggests that human hair locks were also a sign of pledges of allegiance, and horsehair locks pledges of horses (Moore to author, 1989).

Horsehair fringes, often dyed green or yellow, occur not only on early Sioux shirts, such as that collected by Francis Parkman at Fort Laramie in 1846 (Peabody Museum specimen no. 1387), but also on the famous Red Cloud shirt now in the Cody collections; however, <u>black</u> horsehair was sometimes used as a substitute for human hair which related to coups counted (Denig, 1930: 560).

Horse symbolism was also expressed in the carving of horse effigies which were used in re-enacting coups counted in victory dances or they may be carried

Laramie sammelte (Peabody Museum, Exemplar No. 1387), sondern auch an dem berühmten Red Cloud-Hemd, das sich heute in den Cody-Sammlungen befindet. <u>Schwarzes</u> Pferdehaar wurde aber auch manchmal als Ersatz für Menschenhaar in Verbindung mit geschlagenen Coups benutzt (Denig, 1930: 560).

Pferdesymbolismus kam ferner in den Schnitzereien von Pferdefiguren zum Ausdruck, die zur Darstellung von geschlagenen Coups und in Siegestänzen benutzt wurden, oder sie konnten als Erinnerungen an bestimmte Pferde getragen werden, die im Kampf getötet worden waren. All dies unterstreicht die enorme Bedeutung des Pferdes in der Plainsindianerkultur.

as memorials to certain horses killed in battle: all this underlined the enormous importance of the horse in Plains Indian culture.

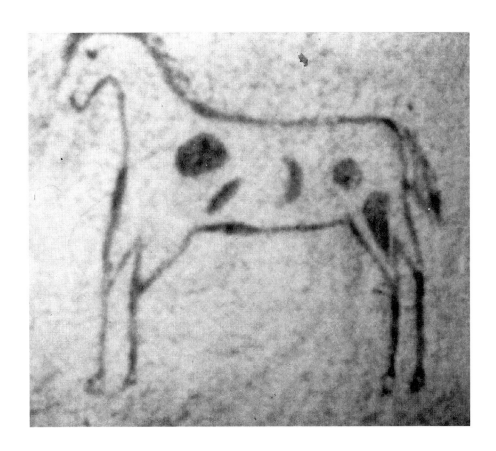

1) Sacred horse, probably Blackfeet, and painted with moon symbols and comet. Museum of Mankind, London. (Specimen no. Q72 AMi4). Photograph by C. F. Taylor.

1) Heiliges Pferd, wahrscheinlich Blackfeet, bemalt mit Mond- und Kometen-Symbolen. Foto von C. F. Taylor.

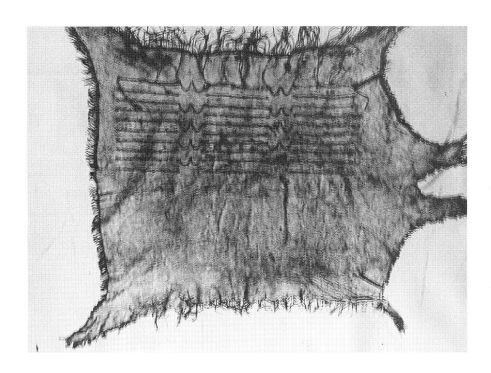

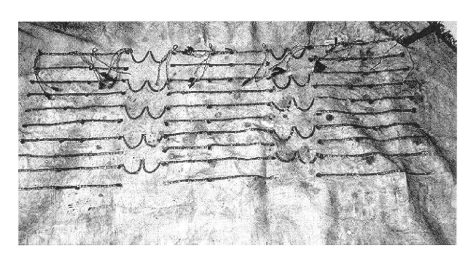

2 + 3) A horse caparison, probably Sioux and dating from circa 1850. (A similar one to this is illustrated in Fig. 15.) Wharncliffe collection, Sheffield Museum, England. (Specimen no. X1978:866). Photograph by C. F. Taylor

2 + 3) Eine Schabracke, wahrscheinlich Sioux, um ca. 1850. (Ein ähnliches Stück ist in Abb. 15 dargestellt.) Wharncliffe-Sammlung, Sheffield Museum, England. Nr. X1978:866. Foto von C. F. Taylor.

Das Erscheinen des Pferdes

Das Pferd hat bekanntermaßen seinen Ursprung nicht in Nordamerika. Die ersten Pferde, die die Indianer des Festlandes zu Gesicht bekamen, waren jene der aus Mexiko eindringenden spanischen Eroberer (Abb. 1a). Wenige Jahre später brachte De Soto das Pferd nach Florida und westwärts zum Mississippi, während Coronado es bei seinem Marsch nach Quivira 1541 bei den Indianern der Great Plains einführte. Das Pferd war bei den Spaniern höchst begehrt, hauptsächlich weil sein Transport in die Neue Welt so schwierig war, und wenn dem Historiker Prescott zu glauben ist, wurde jedes Tier mit 800 bis 1.000 Dollar bewertet. Als Cortez im Februar 1519 bei Cape St. Antonio landete, führte er nur 16 Pferde mit sich, aber er ging berechtigterweise von der großen Bedeutung aus, die die Kavallerie für seine Expedition haben würde, egal wie gering ihre Zahl war, und es wurde später berichtet, daß die Indianer, auf die sie trafen, *„entsetzt über die monströsen Erscheinungen waren, (da) sie annahmen, Reiter und Pferd, die sie nie zuvor gesehen hatten, seien ein und daselbe Wesen"* (Prescott, Kirk ed., 1929: 136) ... wie der Zentaur der griechischen Mythologie.

Auch unter den Pawnee gibt es eine Überlieferung, nach der ihre Vorfahren ein Muli mit einem Reiter für ein Tier hielten, auf das sie aus der Distanz schossen. Erst als der Mann stürzte und sie das Tier einfingen, erkannten sie ihren Irrtum. Es wird ferner zuverlässig berichtet, daß, als Antonio de Espejo 1583 die Hopi besuchte, die Indianer in dem Glauben, daß die Pferde heilig seien, baumwollene Gewänder auf dem Boden ausbreiteten, über die die Tiere schreiten konnten.

Diese sakrale Charakterisierung zeigt sich in den verschiedenen Namen, mit denen das Pferd bezeichnet wurde, so etwa *sun'ka wakan* bei den Lakota, „geheimnisvoller Hund".

Hier ist natürlich nicht der Ort, die Ausbreitung des Pferdes von den spanischen Ansiedlungen im Südwesten nach Norden oder die tatsächlichen unterschiedlichen Zeiträume, in denen die Plateau- und Plainsvölker in seinen Besitz gelangten, zu erörtern. Es ist jedoch angebracht, das Verhalten der Völker die das Pferd erwarben zu untersuchen und wie sie versuchten, sein plötzliches Erscheinen zu rationalisieren.

Die Plateau-Indianer sagen, daß die ersten Pferde, die sie sahen, alle sehr klein waren; und doch fürchteten die ersten Menschen, sie zu reiten, aus Angst herunterzufallen. Offenbar *„ritt der erste Mensch, der ein Pferd bestieg, mit zwei langen Stöcken, einen in jeder Hand, um sich abzustützen. Ein anderer Mann führte das Pferd langsam, und der Reiter bewegte die Stöcke (wie man es mit Spazierstöcken tut) als sie dahinzogen"* (Abb. 2a) Teit, Boas ed., 1930: 250).

The coming of the horse

The horse, of course, is not indigenous to North America, and the first ones seen by the Mainland Indians were those of the Spanish invaders of Mexico (Fig. 1a). A few years later, De Soto brought the horse into Florida and westward to the Mississippi, while Coronado - on his march to Quivira in 1541 - introduced it to the Indians of the Great Plains. The animal was much coveted by the Spaniards mainly because of the difficulty of transportation to the New World, and if the historian, Prescott, is to be believed, each was valued at between $ 800 to $ 1,000 a piece. When Cortez landed at Cape St. Antonio in February 1519, he had with him only sixteen horses, but he rightfully speculated the great importance of the cavalry on his expedition, however small in number, and it was later reported that the Indians they encountered were „*terrified at the monstrous apparition (as) they supposed the rider and the horse, which they had never before seen, to be one and the same*" (Prescott, Kirk ed., 1929: 136) ... as the centaur in Greek mythology.

Among the Pawnee too there is a tradition that their ancestors mistook a mule ridden by a man for a single animal, which they shot at from a distance; not until the man fell and they captured the animal did they realize their mistake! It is also reliably reported that when, in 1583, Antonio de Espejo visited the Hopi, the Indians spread cotton garments on the ground for the horses to walk on, believing that the horses were sacred.

This sacred character is shown in the names given by the Lakota to the horse, such as the Lakota *sun'ka wakan*, „mysterious dog".

This, of course, is not the place to discuss the northward spread of the horse from the Spanish settlements in the southwest, or indeed the various dates of acquisition by the Plateau and Plains people. However, it is appropriate to consider further the reaction of the people who acquired the horse and how they attempted to rationalize its sudden appearance among them.

Plateau Indians say that the earliest horses they saw were all very small; and yet at first people were afraid to ride them for fear of falling off. Apparently, the „*first person who mounted it rode with two long sticks, one in each hand, to steady himself. Another man led the horse slowly, and the rider shifted the sticks (as one does with walking sticks) as they went along*" (Fig. 2a) (Teit, Boas ed., 1930:250).

Die mystische Nation

Bei mehreren Plainsstämmen wurde der Ursprung des Pferdes mit zahlreichen Mythen erklärt, denen zufolge die Pferde aus der Erde, aus Seen oder Quellen oder von der Sonne gekommen waren. Daher stellte John Ewers' Analyse der Blackfeet-Mythen über den Ursprung der Pferde fest, daß ihr Erscheinen als Geschenk des Himmels oder von Unterwassergeistern erklärt wurde, und er schlußfolgerte, daß *„die Pferdeursprungsmythen den Stammesmustern folgen, die den Ursprung der meisten sakralen Besitztümer der einen oder anderen dieser geistigen Quellen zuschreiben"* (Ewers, 1955: 297).

In der Mythe, die erzählt, wie der Donner den Blackfeet die Pferde schenkt, besucht ein Piegan - Wise Man - eine andere Welt, die sich im Besitz des Donners befand, der ihn über den Wert gefärbter Stachelschweinborsten zur Verzierung von Kleidungsstücken unterrichtete - und dabei den sakralen Charakter dieser Kunstform hervorhob -, von der Kraft von mit Tieren bemalten Zelten und vom Gebrauch der Heiligen Pfeifen. Schließlich unterwies er Wise Man, die Schwänze zweier Pferde zusammenzuknoten und sie mit sich zurück auf die Erde zu nehmen.[1] Ähnliche Mythen gibt es bei den Lakota. So berichtet Wissler, daß das Pferd als Kreatur von rätselhaftem Ursprung stets begehrenswert für sie war, und häufig wurde angenommen, es sei ein Geschenk des Donners. In jedem Fall, sagte er, gab es in der Vorstellung der Lakota eine Verbindung zwischen der Kraft des Kriegspferdes und dem Donner (Wissler, 1907: 193), und die Pferde wurden in den Rang eines mystischen Volkes erhoben.

Bei den Assiniboin gab es eine noch stärkere Verbindung zwischen dem neuen Tier und dem Menschen; denn eine ihrer Mythen erzählt, daß Trickster - ihr großer Kulturheros - sowohl den Menschen als auch die Pferde aus Erde erschuf (Penney and Stouffer, 1986: 21, und Lowie, 1909: 57-58).

Geschichten dieser Art, so schlußfolgerte Ewers, *„sind der Beweis, daß in der Vorstellung der Eingeborenen das Pferd ein bedeutendes Gottesgeschenk war, ebenso wie ihre heiligsten Zeremonien, erschaffen von denselben übernatürlichen Mächten, die den Indianern ihre traditionellen zeremoniellen Einrichtungen verliehen hatten"* (Ewers, 1955: 297-8).

---

[1] Nachdem ich diese Vorlesung gehalten hatte, erzählte mir Stuart Conner von der Felszeichnung von einem zweiköpfigen Pferd nahe Joliet, Montana. Reference Code 24.CB.402.

The mystical nation

Among several Plains tribes, the origin of the horse was explained by a number of myths representing horses as coming out of the earth, from lakes or springs, or from the sun. Thus, John Ewers' analysis of Blackfeet myths relating to the origin of horses among that tribe, found that their appearance was explained in terms of a gift from the sky or underwater spirits and in this respect he concluded that „*the horse origin myths follow the tribal pattern of imputing the origin of their most sacred possessions to one or the other of these spirit sources*" (Ewers, 1955: 297).

In the myth relating to Thunder's gift of horses to the Blackfeet, a Piegan - Wise Man - visits another world occupied by Thunder who tells him of the value of dyed porcupine quills for decorating garments (underlining the sacred nature of this art form), the power of animal painted lodges and the use of sacred pipes. Finally, he instructed Wise Man to tie the tails of two horses together, and take them back to earth.[1] Similar myths occur with the Lakota. Thus, Wissler reported that the horse always appealed to them as a creature of mysterious origin, and in many cases was assumed to have been given by the thunder. In any event, he said that there was an association in the Lakota mind between the power of the war horse and the thunder (Wissler, 1907: 193), and the horse was elevated to the status of a mystical nation.

For the Assiniboin, there was an even stronger relationship between this new beast and man since one of their myths relates that Trickster - their great culture hero -created both men and horses from the dirt of the earth (Penney and Stouffer, 1986: 21 and Lowie, 1909: 57-58).

Stories of this sort, Ewers concluded, „*constitute evidence that to the native mind, the horse was a godsend of importance comparable to that of their most sacred ceremonies, created by the same supernatural powers who gave the Indians their traditional ceremonial institutions*" (Ewers, 1955: 297-8).

---

[1] After this lecture Stuart Conner told me of a two headed horse petroglyph near Joliet, Montana. Reference code 24.CB.402.

Pferdebilder

Zu den frühesten uns zur Verfügung stehenden Pferdeabbildungen gehören Felszeichnungen an verschiedenen Plätzen überall im Plainsgebiet. Beispielsweise wurden an dem berühmten Writing-on-Stone-Platz in Süd-Alberta mehr als 250 Pferdebilder an 41 Stellen festgestellt (Keyser, 1977: 15). Einige der frühesten Pferdedarstellungen waren extrem vereinfacht, aber viele Details, die auf Ausrüstungsstücke und Methoden der Kriegsführung hinweisen, sind gut illustriert. (Abb. 3a) Insbesondere bei den frühen Piktographien jedoch stellt sich gelegentlich die Frage, was der Künstler versucht hat, darzustellen. Man beachte (Abb. 4 a) die grünen Parallellinien auf den menschlichen Gestalten und Pferden - sollen diese das Skelett darstellen, oder was? Ferner wird aus unerklärlichen Gründen die Herzlinie - die so oft bei anderen Tieren zu sehen ist - selten gezeichnet, obwohl es einige bemerkenswerte Ausnahmen gibt, wie etwa in Abb. 4 b zu sehen.
Diese Piktographie befindet sich auf einer alten Northern Plains-Robe - wahrscheinlich Blackfeet -, die heute im *Musée de l'Homme* in Paris liegt. Manchmal waren Pferdeabbildungen so dramatisch und symbolträchtig, daß man überwältigt ist von den Fähigkeiten und der gedanklichen Kraft des Künstlers (Abb. 4c).

Mit dem Fortschreiten der Zeit, wurde das Pferd immer realistischer wiedergegeben - nicht nur in Piktographien, sondern auch in Schnitzereien in Holz und Stein, und bis ins 20. Jahrhundert wird die mystische Natur des Tieres betont, etwa in dem höchst phantasievollen Gemälde eines Dakota-Pferdes von Oscar Howe (Abb. 5), das eine Mischung aus Realismus und Abstraktion zeigt.

Zu anderen Zeiten wurde das Pferd dreidimensional, in dramatischer Bewegung mit fliegender Mähne und zurückgebogenen Ohren dargestellt, und dann einmal - diesmal in stiller Schönheit - in Ruhe. (Abb. 6 a + b) (Penney and Stouffer, 1986: 23)

Horse images

Among the earliest illustrations which we have of horses, of course, are their appearance in the Rock Art at various sites across the Plains. At the famous Writing-on-Stone site in Southern Alberta, for example, more than two hundred and fifty horse images are recorded at forty-one sites (Keyser, 1977:15). Some of the earliest renderings of horses were extremely rudimentary but many details relating to accoutrements used and modes of warfare, are well illustrated (Fig. 3a). However, especially with the early pictographs, one sometimes wonders just what the artist was attempting to depict. Note (Fig. 4 a) the green parallel lines on both human figures and horse - is this meant to convey the skeleton or what? Also, for some unaccountable reason, the heart line (used so often with other animals) is seldom depicted, although there are some notable exceptions, such as that shown in Fig. 4 b. This pictograph is from an ancient Northern Plains - probably Blackfeet - robe now in the *Musée de l'Homme*, Paris. Sometimes, horse images were so dramatic and symbolic, that one is overawed by the skill and complex thoughts of the artist (Fig. 4c).

So clearly as time passed, it was rendered in a more realistic fashion - not only in pictographs but also in carvings both in wood and stone, and well into the twentieth century the theme of the mystical nature of the animal is emphasized, such as in this highly imaginative painting of a Dakota horse by Oscar Howe (Fig. 5), where we have a combination of realism and abstract composition.

At other times, the horse was rendered three dimensionally in dramatic motion with flying mane and back-turned ears, and still again - but this time in quiet beauty - at rest.(Figs. 6 a + b) (Penney and Stouffer, 1986: 23)

Übernatürliche Kräfte

Das Pferd hatte offensichtlich enormen Einfluß auf die Lebensweise jener zu Fuß gehenden Nomaden, die die Plains durchstreiften und bis dahin den Hund als Transportmittel benutzt hatten. Mit dem Erwerb des Pferdes konnten weitaus größere Ladungen mitgeführt werden; so wurden die Tipis größer, die Jagdtechniken wechselten, die Camps wurden häufiger verlegt und der Bewegungsspielraum wurde größer. Auch die Zahl der Besitztümer, die transportiert werden konnten, nahm zu, und Kriegsführung, Handel, Freizeitbeschäftigungen und das gemeinschaftliche Leben änderten sich dramatisch - mit einem Wort, die Kultur wurde „üppiger". Aber, höchst bedeutungsvoll, religiöse und sakrale Überzeugungen wurden ebenfalls modifiziert, um das Pferd in die neue, höchst mobile Kultur einzubeziehen.

Anscheinend gibt es nur wenige Beweise für die Annahme, daß vor den Pferdetagen der Hund - zu dieser Zeit das wichtigste Lasttier - irgendwelche ausgedehnten sakralen Verbindungen hatte, obwohl berichtet wird, daß bei der Übertragung der Long Time Pipe der Blood-Indianer die Bezahlung in Hunden erfolgte (Ewers, 1955: 289). Dagegen nahm das Pferd eine bemerkenswert herausragende Position in den religiösen Überzeugungen und Ritualen der Plainsindianer ein. (Fig. 7) Das plötzliche Erscheinen dieses Tieres, das die Lebensqualität so sehr verbesserte, wurde in ihrer Mythologie als Geschenk höherer Mächte dargestellt, und es hatte weitreichenden Einfluß auf ihre religiösen und mythologischen Konzepte.

Wie Penney festgestellt hat, glauben viele Plainsindianer, daß Pferde übernatürliche Fähigkeiten besaßen, ähnlich denen anderer starker Tiere wie Wapiti und Bison (Penney and Stouffer, 1986: 20). Das Pferd war jedoch in mannigfacher Weise einzigartig. Im Gegensatz zu anderen großen Tieren flüchtete es nicht vor den Menschen und gestattete es, auf seinem Rücken zu reiten, so daß es schließlich mit der Lebensweise der Plainsindianer verflochten und für sie unentbehrlich wurde. Seine weitere Einzigartigkeit wurde von einem anderen charakteristischen Merkmal unterstrichen, das es unübersehbar von allen anderen Tieren unterschied, die die Indianer vorher gekannt hatten, und das war sein ungeteilter Fuß. (Abb. 8) Wapiti, Bison und Hirsch hatten vier Zehen an jedem Fuß, die Antilope zwei, was schon ziemlich bemerkenswert war, aber das Pferd - wunderbar, wie es ihnen erscheinen mußte - hatte nur einen, und es war diese Besonderheit, die seine Spur allein für sich genommen so kennzeichnend machte, daß der Künstler darauf hinzuweisen versuchte, indem er die <u>Fährte</u> des Tieres am Ende des Beines festmachte, als ein Symbol, es ohne jeden Zweifel unterscheiden zu können, mehr als der Versuch einer realistischen Darstellung des Hufs (Smith, 1943: 113-4). In späteren Jahren wurde dieses Symbol modifiziert, als die Stämme auf die Weißen trafen, die beschlagene Pferde ritten, und das Hufmotiv wurde unterschiedlich dargestellt (Fig. 9).

Noch unzweifelhafter stieß John Ewers während seiner Feldforschungen bei den Blackfeet in den 1940er Jahren auf die allgemeine Überzeugung, daß

Supernatural powers

The horse clearly had an enormous impact on the lifestyle of those pedestrian nomads who roamed the Plains and previously used the dog for transportation. With the acquisition of the horse far bigger loads could be carried, thus tipis increased in size, techniques of hunting changed, the frequency of camp movements increased, as well as range of movement. The number of possessions which could be transported also increased, and warfare, trade, recreation and social life, were all changed dramatically - in a word, the culture was „magnified". But, most significantly, religious and sacred beliefs were also modified to incorporate the horse into the new and highly mobile culture.

There seems to be little evidence to suggest that prior to horse days, the dog - which was then the principal beast of burden - had any widespread sacred associations, although in the transfer of the Blood Indians' Long Time Pipe, it is recorded that dog payments were made (Ewers, 1955: 289). In contrast, the horse came to occupy a position of considerable prominence in the Plains Indians' religious beliefs and rituals (Fig. 7). The sudden appearance of this animal which so improved the quality of life, was referred to in their mythology as a gift from higher powers and it had a far reaching influence in their religious and mythological concepts.

As Penney has pointed out, many Plains tribes believed that horses possessed supernatural abilities similar to those of other powerful animals, such as the elk and buffalo (Penney and Stouffer, 1986: 20). It was, however, unique in more ways than one. Unlike other large animals, it did not shy away from humans and allowed a person to ride upon its back, so that ultimately the animal became intertwined in and indispensable to, the Plains Indians' lifeway. Its further uniqueness was underlined by another distinctive feature which set it clearly apart from all other animals the Indians had previously known, and that was its undivided foot (Fig. 8). The elk, buffalo and deer had four toes to each foot, the antelope two, which was sufficiently remarkable, but the horse, wonderful as it must have seemed, had only one, and it was this peculiarity - revealing itself so strikingly in its track - which the artist sought to indicate by attaching the animal's track to the end of the leg, as a symbol to distinguish it beyond question, rather than attempt a realistic portrayal of the hoof as it appears in nature (Smith, 1943: 113-4). In later years, this symbol was modified when tribes came up against whites who had shod horses, and the hoof motif was rendered differently (Fig. 9).

More specifically, during his fieldwork among the Blackfeet in the 1940s, John Ewers found that there was a general belief that horses possessed supernatural powers, and just as they believed some humans possessed stronger supernatural powers than others, so they thought that the sacred powers of some horses were more potent than those of ordinary horses. Thus *„horses that performed deeds of unusual strength or endurance, that miraculously escaped from battle without a scratch, or received wounds thought to have been mortal yet recovered, were spoken of by informants as animals possessing potent 'secret power'.*

Pferde übernatürliche Kräfte besaßen, und genauso wie geglaubt wurde, daß einige Menschen über stärkere übernatürliche Kräfte verfügten als andere, so wurde angenommen, daß die sakralen Kräfte einiger Pferde stärker waren als die einfacher Pferde. So wurde von *„Pferden, die Taten von ungewöhnlicher Kraft oder Ausdauer vollbracht hatten, die wunderbarerweise ohne Verletzung aus einer Schlacht entkommen waren, oder die scheinbar tödliche Wunden empfangen hatten und sich dennoch erholten, von Informanten als von Tieren gesprochen, die eine starke „geheime Kraft" besaßen. Ihre bemerkenswerten Taten waren für die Indianer der Beweis für den Besitz dieser Kraft... Wie auch bei Menschen wurde geglaubt, daß Pferde den Tod als Geister überlebten und die Fähigkeit besaßen, zurückzukehren und ihre geistige Gegenwart den Lebenden zu manifestieren"* (Ewers, 1955: 290-1).

Daher wurden gelegentlich die bevorzugten Pferde nach dem Tod ihres Besitzers geopfert, so daß die enge Kameradschaft, die zwischen Mensch und Pferd im Leben existiert hatte, *„sich in der Geisterwelt fortsetzen konnte"* (ibid: 284).

Von den Blackfeet wird berichtet, daß das Lieblingspferd eines toten Mannes, ausgestattet mit üppigem und kostbarem Sattelzeug, bemalt mit Piktographien, die die Coups des Besitzers darstellten, den Schweif geflochten und mit Federanhängern geschmückt, am Grab des Besitzers erschossen wurde. Die Überzeugung war, daß der Geist des Pferdes sich, mit allen Insignien, die es trug, als es getötet wurde, mit dem seines Besitzers vereinigte (ibid: 285).

Maximilian berichtete, daß ihm von Fällen erzählt wurde, als *„zwölf oder fünfzehn Pferde ... bei der Bestattung eines verehrten Häuptlings getötet wurden"* (Maximilian, Thwaites, ed., 1906, vol. XIII: 121). Dieser Brauch war auf den Plains weit verbreitet (Abb. 10), und in einigen Fällen kam es zu furchtbaren Übertreibungen. So wurde gesagt, daß nach dem Tod eines führenden Kiowa-Häuptlings über 70 Pferde getötet wurden. Dies war jedoch unüblich, und der Brauch, Mähne und Schweif des Pferdes eines toten Mannes zu stutzen war, wie es scheint, ebenfalls eine übliche Sitte, den Toten zu ehren, *„ohne wertvollen Besitz zu opfern"* (Ewers, 1955: 287).

Their remarkable deeds were proof to the Indians of their possession of that power... Like humans, horses were believed to survive death as spirits possessing the power to return and make their spirit presences known to the living" (Ewers, 1955: 290-1).

Thus, sometimes favorite horses were sacrificed after the death of the owner so that the close companionship which existed between man and horse in life *„might continue in the spirit world"* (ibid: 284).

It is reported for the Blackfeet that the dead man's favorite horse, equipped with elaborate and costly riding gear, painted with pictographs representing the owner's coups, its tail braided and decorated with a feather pendant, was shot at the grave of its owner, the belief being that the spirit of the horse joined that of its owner, wearing the trappings which it bore at the time it was killed (ibid: 285).

Maximilian reported that he was told of instances when *„twelve or fifteen horses were killed ... at the funeral of a celebrated chief"* (Maximilian, Thwaites ed., 1906. Vol. XXIII: 121). The custom was widespread across the Plains (Fig. 10), and in some cases the extravagance was staggering. Thus, over seventy horses were said to have been killed after the death of a leading Kiowa chief. However, this was unusual, and the custom of cropping the mane and tail of a dead man's horse or horses was, it appears, also a common way of honoring the dead *„without sacrificing valuable property"*, (Ewers, 1955: 287).

Pferde-Medizin-Kraft

Herausragend unter den neuen religiösen Veränderungen war das Entstehen von Pferde-Medizin-Gesellschaften (Abb. 11), über die wegen der Heimlichkeit, die sie umgab, nur wenige Berichte in der anthropologischen Literatur verfügbar sind - obwohl sie offensichtlich auf den Plains und darüber hinaus weit verbreitet waren.

Pferdemedizinmännern wurden weitreichende mannigfaltige Kräfte zugeschrieben, die sie in einem Traum oder einer Vision erlangt hatten. Ein Beispiel war Wolf Calf, der als Urheber des Pferdemedizinkults bei den Piegan angesehen wurde. Er hatte seine Kenntnisse über Wurzeln und Kräuter von einem wilden Pferd und seinem eigenen Lieblingshengst erhalten. Ihm war nicht nur die Kraft gegeben worden, kranke Pferde zu heilen, sondern auch Menschen, und er wandte bestimmte Kräuter und Rituale an, um das Wetter zu beeinflussen (ibid: 259).

Ein typisches Pferdekultzeremoniell wurde von John Ewers berichtet, der daran nahe Browning im Frühling 1943 teilnahm. Die Zeremonie, die zugunsten einer jungen Frau abgehalten wurde, die sich seit einiger Zeit in schlechtem gesundheitlichen Zustand befand, dauerte über sieben Stunden. Im Mittelpunkt stand ein zeremonieller Erdaltar. Dieser wurde angelegt, indem graue Erde auf ein kreisförmiges Stück Stoff von etwa 30 Zoll Durchmesser gestreut wurde. In dessen Mitte war ein Quadrat mit zwei Hälften in Schwarz und Rot gemalt. (Abb. 12) Schwarze und rote Federn waren an jeder Ecke des Quadrats plaziert.

Wallace Night Gun (Abb. 13), dem die Zeremonie von ihrem Urheber, Wolf Calf, gelehrt worden war, erklärte, daß der Aufbau des Altars entsprechend einem von Wolf Calfs Träumen erfolgte und daß es wichtig war, daß *„er in genau dieser Weise für jede Pferdetanzzeremonie angelegt wurde"* (ibid: 266). Es wurde erklärt, daß das rote Rechteck den Tag und das schwarze die Nacht symbolisierte, während die Zickzack-Furchen *„des Donners Blitz"* darstellten, und die Federn an den Ecken wurden jenen gegeben, die um seine Hilfe nachgesucht hatten - sie mußten daher von Zeit zu Zeit erneuert werden (ibid).

Ein Rohhautausschnitt in Form eines Pferdes, etwa 6,5 Zoll lang[2], spielte eine herausragende Rolle in der Zeremonie und wurde benutzt, um Pferdemedizinmänner davor zu schützen, jemals über einen Felsen zu stürzen oder sich daran zu stoßen[3]. Sein Geist wurde angebetet, und der Leiter, Wallace Night Gun, tanzte darauf zu, ein geflochtenes Rohhautseil und eine Peitsche haltend, die er aus dem Pferdemedizinbündel genommen hatte. Dann wurden

---

[2] Wurde auch von den Hidatsa benutzt. *„Er konnte die Gestalt eines Mannes auf die Brust seines Ponies malen oder eine grobe Figur eines Reiters zu Pferde ausschneiden und eines Mannes aus Pappe, Blech oder Holz"* (Brief von Arnie Brownstone an C. F. T., 2. 12. 1993) (Hidatsa Mandan Report. Fort Berthold Reservation, 1918, Vol. 22: 235).

[3] Es gab einen starken Bezug zum praktischen Aspekt des Pferdegebrauchs. Daher spielte der Bezug zu gebrochenen Knochen eine herausragende Rolle in der Zeremonie.

Horse medicine power

Prominent in the new religious innovations, was the development of Horse Medicine Societies (Fig. 11) which because of the secrecy which surrounded them, have received only limited reportage in the anthropological literature - although it was clearly widely diffused across the Plains and beyond.

Horse Medicine Men were credited with widely varying powers, having obtained this power in a dream or vision. Typical was that of Wolf Calf who was credited as being the originator of the horse medicine cult among the Piegan having received knowledge of roots and herbs from a wild horse and his own favorite stallion. He was given the power not only to cure sick horses but also humans and used certain herbs and rituals to influence the weather (ibid: 259).

A typical horse cult ceremonial has been reported on by John Ewers who attended one near Browning in the spring of 1943. The ceremonial was for the benefit of a young woman who had been in poor health for some time and it lasted more than seven hours. The central focus was a ceremonial earth altar made by spreading grey earth onto a cloth in the form of a circle some 30 inches in diameter, at the center of which was drawn a square with two halves in black and red. (Fig. 12) Black and red feathers were placed at each corner of the square.

Wallace Night Gun (Fig. 13) - who had been taught the ceremonial by its originator, Wolf Calf - explained that the construction of the altar was in accordance with one of Wolf Calf's dreams, and that it was important that „*it should be made in just that way for every horse dance ceremony*" (ibid: 266). It was explained that the red rectangle symbolized day and the black one, night. While zigzag furrows represented the „*thunder's lightning*" and plumes at the corners were given to those who had requested his help - thus, they had to be renewed from time to time (ibid.).

A rawhide cut-out of a horse some 6.5 inches (165 mm)long[2], figured prominently in the ceremonial and it was used to caution Horse Medicine Men never to fall over or bump a rock[3]; its spirit was prayed to and the leader, Wallace Night Gun, danced towards it holding a braided rawhide rope and whip which he had taken from the Horse Medicine Bundle. Prayers were then made for the sick for whom the ceremonial was performed.

The whole ceremonial followed the pattern of other Blackfeet rituals - singing, drumming, dancing with sacred paraphernalia, praying, the passing of the pipe, face painting, the recognition of taboos and the use of dry-painted altars. There was, however, one difference. In all the ceremonial there was

---

[2] Also used by Hidatsa. „ *He might paint a man's body on his pony's breast or cut out a rude figure of a man or a horse and a man out of pasteboard, tin or wood*" (Letter Arni Brownstone to C. F. T., 2. 12. 1993) (Hidatsa-Mandan Report, Fort Berthold Reservation, 1918. Vol. 22: 295).

[3] There was much reference to the practical aspect of horse handling. Thus, reference to broken bones figures prominently in the ceremonial.

Gebete für die Kranke gesprochen, für die die Zeremonie durchgeführt wurde.

Das gesamte Zeremoniell folgte dem Muster anderer Blackfeet-Rituale - es wurde gesungen, die Trommel geschlagen, mit sakralen Gegenständen getanzt, gebetet, die Pfeife kreiste, die Gesichter wurden bemalt, Tabus beachtet, und es wurden trockengemalte Altäre benutzt. Es gab jedoch einen Unterschied: In der gesamten Zeremonie wurde das Ritual einheitlich angewandt und dreimal wiederholt, was markant mit anderen Zeremonien kontrastierte, bei denen 4 die Norm war.

Herausragend in diesem Zeremoniell war die Verwendung des Medizinbündels, das Rohhaut und perlenbesetzte Pferdefetische, Kräuter, Federn, Seile, Pfeifenköpfe und Reitpeitschen enthielt. Mit diesen Gegenständen wurde mit größter Sorgfalt umgegangen.

Bei manchen Gelegenheiten nahmen Pferde an den heiligsten religiösen Zeremonien der Sioux teil. Abb. 14 zeigt eine Sioux-Piktographie eines Kriegers, der an einem Sonnentanz teilnimmt und von seinem Pferd begleitet wird. Die Legende der Zeichnung erklärt, daß der Krieger und sein Pferd zugunsten der Gemeinschaft tanzen, um die Zahl der Pferde zu vergrößern und den erfolgreichen Kampf gegen Feinde zu sichern (siehe Penney and Stouffer, 1986: 20).[4]

---

[4] Ähnlich bei den Blackfeet, wo ein Pferdefetisch eine herausragende Rolle spielte.

repeated and consistent employment of the ritual number three, which contrasted markedly with other ceremonials where four was the norm.

Prominent in this ceremonial was the use of the Medicine Bundle which contained rawhide and beaded horse fetishes, herbs, feathers, ropes, pipe bowls and quirts. Great emphasis was put on handling them with care.

On occasions horses sometimes joined the performers in the most sacred of Sioux religious ceremonies. Fig. 14 shows a Sioux pictograph of a warrior accompanied by his horse and participating in the Sun-dance. An explanatory note above the drawing explains that the warrior and his horse are dancing in order to benefit the community, increase the herd of horses and ensure succesful combat over the enemy (See Penney and Stouffer, 1986: 20).[4]

---

[4] As with the Blackfeet a horse fetish figures prominently.

1 a) Among the first horses seen by American Indians were those brought in by the Spanish invaders to Mexico. This petroglyph is on the walls of Massacre Cave in the Canyon del Muerto, Arizona, and dates from the early nineteenth century.

1 a) Die ersten Pferde, die amerikanische Indianer sahen, waren jene, die von den spanischen Invasoren nach Mexiko gebracht wurden. Diese Petroglyphe befindet sich an den Wänden der Massacre Cave im Canyon del Muerto (Arizona) und datiert ins frühe 19. Jahrhundert.

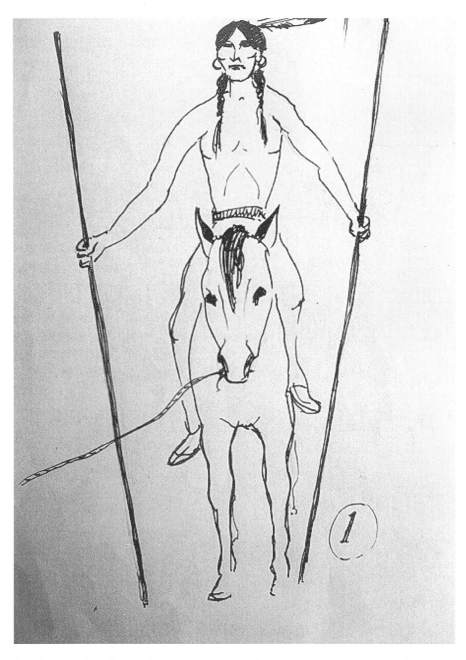

2 a) Plateau Indians first used sticks to stop them falling off the horse. Sketch after a description in Teit (Boas ed., 1930: 250). Courtesy Ian West and San Cahoon.

2 a) Die Plateau-Indianer benutzten anfangs Stöcke, um ein Herunterfallen vom Pferd zu verhindern. Skizze nach einer Beschreibung in Teit. (Boas ed. 1930: 250.) Mit Genehmigung von Ian West und San Cahoon.

3 a) Horse armor and shield-bearing warrior, probably eighteenth century at Writing-on-Stone site, Southern Alberta, Canada. (After Keyser, 1987: 47).

3 a) Pferdepanzerung und schildtragender Krieger, wahrscheinlich 18. Jahrhundert, vom Writing-on-Stone-Gelände, Süd-Alberta, Kanada. (Nach Keyser, 1987: 47.)

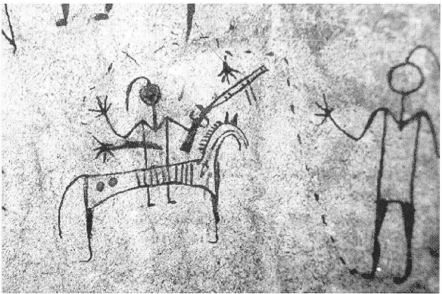

4 a + 4 b) Two images from a buffalo robe in the Musée de l'Homme, Paris, dating from <u>at least</u> 1830 and from the Northern Plains. (Specimen no. 96.73.1). (a) green parallel lines on horse and female figure possibly represents the skeleton. (b) the heart line on a horse - a fairly rare feature on horses.

4 a + 4 b) Zwei Bilder von einer Bisonrobe im Musée de l'Homme, Paris. <u>Mindestens</u> von 1830, von den nördlichen Plains. Nr. 96.73.1. (a) Grüne Parallellinien auf dem Pferd und der weiblichen Gestalt stellen möglicherweise das Skelett dar. (b) Die Herzlinie auf einem Pferd - eine ziemlich seltene Darstellung auf Pferden.

4 c) Pictographic drawing showing a dream vision of Black Hawk a Sans Arc Medicine Man, circa 1880, riding a mythical „buffalo horse eagle". (Private collection)

4 c) Piktographische Zeichnung einer Traumvision von Blawk Hawk, einem Sans Arc-Medizinmann, ca. 1880. Er reitet einen mythologischen „Büffel-Pferde-Adler". (Privatsammlung)

5) *Sun'ka Wakan*, a „mystical" Dakota horse. Casein by Oscar Howe, 1966. Photograph, courtesy University of South Dakota, Vermillion.

5) *Sun'ka Wakan*, ein „mystisches" Pferd der Dakota. Casein von Oscar Howe, 1966. Foto mit Genehmigung der University of South Dakota, Vermillion.

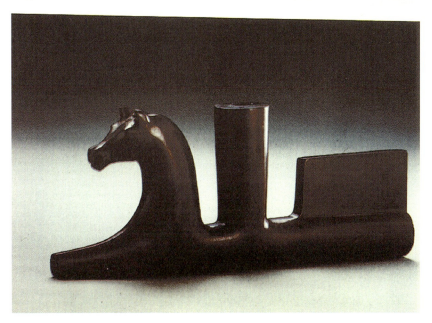

6 a + 6 b) The rendering of a horse in (a) dramatic motion, as in warfare (Eastern Sioux, c. 1880) and (b) at rest in quiet beauty (Cheyenne, c. 1875). Both pipes are in the Detroit Institute of Arts (Specimen nos. 81.490 and 81.242). (See Penney and Stouffer, 1986: 23).

6 a + 6 b) Darstellung eines Pferdes in (a) dramatischer Bewegung, wie etwa im Krieg (Eastern Sioux, ca. 1880) und (b) in Ruhe in stiller Schönheit (Cheyenne, ca. 1875). Beide Stücke befinden sich im Detroit Institute of Arts. Nr. 81.490 und 81.242. (Siehe Penney und Stouffer, 1986: 23.)

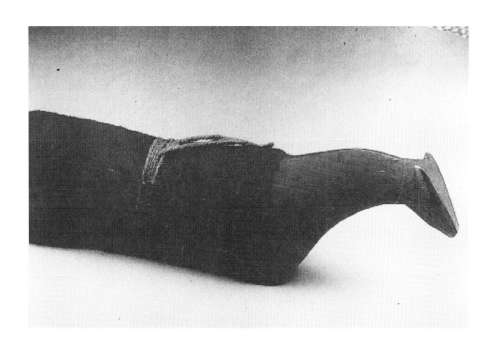

7) The horse occupied considerable prominence in Plains and Prairie religious beliefs. This is a Potawatomi horse effigy, c. 1870, which belonged to a religious practitioner and was used in healing ceremonials. (See Penney and Stouffer, 1986: 19).

7) Das Pferd erhielt bemerkenswerte Bedeutung in den religiösen Überzeugungen auf den Plains und Prärien. Dies ist eine Pferdefigur der Potawatomi, ca. 1870, die einem religiösen Heilkundigen gehörte und in Heilungszeremonien benutzt wurde. (Siehe Penney und Stouffer, 1986: 19.)

8) A Pawnee pictograph showing the hoof print at the extremity of the legs. The undivided foot of the horse was unique among Plains animals. Figure from a watercolor by Titian Ramsay Peale, the original of which is in the Rare Book and Manuscript Library of Yale University. c. 1820. (Courtesy Paul Ritner)

8) Eine Pawnee-Piktographie, die den Hufabdruck am Ende der Beine zeigt. Der ungeteilte Fuß des Pferdes war einzig unter den Tieren der Plains. Teil eines Aquarells von Titian Ramsay Peale. Das Original befindet sich in der Rare Book and Manuscript Library der Yale University, ca. 1820. (Mit Genehmigung von Paul Ritner.)

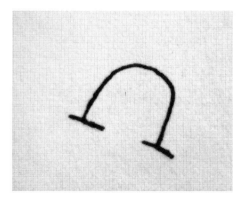

9) The Sioux symbol for shod horses. This is from a Winter Count now in the Museum of Mankind, London, and represents the year 1803-04. (See Howard, 1979).

9) Sioux-Symbol für beschlagene Pferde. Skizze von einem Winter Count, der sich im Museum of Mankind, London, befindet. Das Symbol repräsentiert das Jahr 1803-04. (Siehe Howard, 1979).

10) The „Voice of the Great Spirit", a somewhat romanticized painting of a Crow scaffold burial showing the sacrificed horses. Painting by J. H. Sharp, c. 1900. The original is now in the National Collection of Fine Arts, Smithsonian Institution, Washington D. C.

10) „Die Stimme des Großen Geistes", ein etwas romantisiertes Gemälde einer Crow-Gerüstbestattung, das die geopferten Pferde zeigt. Gemälde von J. H. Sharp, ca. 1900. National Collection of Fine Arts, Smithsonian Institution, Washington D. C.

11) Blackfeet Weather Dancer's shirt, c. 1865. Note the beaded horse effigy attached to the front of this shirt. Horse medicine power could be, among a variety of other things, used to influence the weather. This piece is now in the Denver Art Museum, Denver, Colorado. (Cat. No. 1938.257).

11) Hemd eines Wettertänzers der Blackfeet, ca. 1865. Man beachte die perlenbesetzte Pferdedarstellung, die vorn an diesem Hemd befestigt ist. Pferdemedizinkraft konnte, neben vielerlei anderer Dinge, benutzt werden, um das Wetter zu beeinflussen. Das Stück befindet sich im Denver Art Museum, Denver, Colorado. (Katalog Nr. 1938.257)

12) A Blackfeet horse cult altar, such as that described in Wissler (1911). These altars could be used in ceremonials to improve the health of sick people. (Provincial Museum, Edmonton, Canada).

12) Ein Pferdekultaltar der Blackfeet, wie er in Wissler (1911) beschrieben ist. Diese Altäre konnten in Zeremonien zur Verbesserung des Zustands Kranker verwendet werden. (Provincial Museum, Edmonton, Canada

13) Wallace Night Gun, who was an active member of the Blackfeet horse cult ceremonial. In this ceremonial, there was repeated and consistent employment of the ritual number three. (See Ewers, 1955).

13) Wallace Night Gun, ein aktiver Teilnehmer des Pferdekultzeremoniell der Blackfeet. Dieses Zeremoniell wurde auf der Grundlage der rituellen Zahl drei wiederholt und ständig angewandt. (Siehe Ewers, 1955.)

14) Sioux (Lakota) drawing showing a horse which participated in the Sun-dance. At times, horses joined performers in the religious ceremonials. (Original in the Detroit Institute of Arts. (Specimen no. 81.233.7). See Penney and Stouffer, 1986: 18).

14) Sioux (Lakota)-Zeichnung eines Pferdes, das am Sonnentanz teilgenommen hatte. Manchmal begleiteten Pferde die Teilnehmer an religiösen Zeremonien. (Detroit Institute of Arts. Nr. 81.233.7. Siehe Penney und Stouffer, 1986: 18)

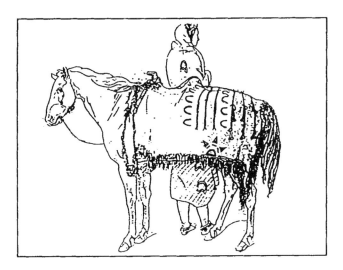

15) A caparison on a Sioux woman's horse. Sketch by Rudolph Kurz, 1851. (Historisches Museum, Bern, Switzerland). These are rare items and only one has been located to date in the ethnographical collections. (See Figs. 2 and 3).

15) Eine Schabracke auf dem Pferd einer Sioux-Frau. Skizze von Rudolph Kurz, 1851. (Historisches Museum, Bern, Schweiz) Es handelt sich um seltene Stücke, und nur eins konnte bisher in den ethnographischen Sammlungen lokalisiert werden. (Siehe Abb. 2 und 3.)

16) Detail of Sioux caparison shown in Fig. 15. This is in the Wharncliffe collection, Sheffield City Museum, Sheffield, England. (Specimen no. 1978.866). It probably dates from c. 1850.

16) Detail der Sioux-Schabracke in Abb. 15. Diese befindet sich in der Wharncliffe-Sammlung, Sheffield City Museum, Sheffield, England. (Nr. 1978.866.) Wahrscheinlich stammt sie von ca. 1850.

17) Spanish horse armor, detail from a painting of escorted Franciscan friars leaving San Carlos Borromeo, c. 1800. Original now in the Society of Californian Pioneers. Such armor styles undoubtedly influenced Plains Indians. (See also Fig. 3 a).

17) Spanische Pferderüstung, Detail eines Gemäldes, auf dem franziskanische Ordensbrüder beim Verlassen von San Carlos Borromeo eskortiert werden, ca. 1800. Diese Art der Panzerung beeinflußte zweifellos die Plainsindianer. (Siehe auch Abb. 3a.)

18) The Plains Indian warshirt concept probably derived from the multilayered buckskin shirts which were used by Plains Indians in pre-gun days. Both horse and rider were covered.

18) Die Kriegshemdkonzeption der Plainsindianer stammte wahrscheinlich von den aus mehreren Lagen bestehenden Hirschlederhemden, die von den Plainsindianern vor dem Auftauchen der Feuerwaffen benutzt wurden. Pferd und Reiter waren bedeckt.

19) A sketch by the Sioux historian, Amos Bad Heart Bull, showing a <u>tailored</u> caparison used on a horse. (See Blish, 1967: 432). Such covers went over the saddle and withers of the horse. Compare with the Kurz sketch (Fig. 15).

19) Skizze des Sioux-Historikers Amos Bad Heart Bull, die eine <u>zugeschnittene</u> Schabracke im Gebrauch auf einem Pferd zeigt. (Siehe Blish, 1967: 432) Solche Decken reichten über Sattel und Widerrist des Pferdes. Vgl. mit der Kurz-Skizze (Abb. 15).

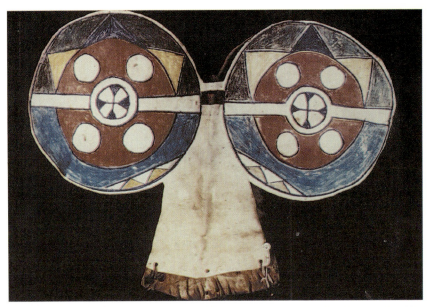

20) Horse „shield" almost certainly Crow. This may be the same as that shown in Fig. 22. (Courtesy Laura Fisher Collection).

20) Pferde-"Schild", höchstwahrscheinlich Crow. Es könnte dasselbe Stück sein, das in Abb. 22 gezeigt wird. (Mit Genehmigung der Laura Fisher Collection.)

22) Crow girl on horseback showing a horse „shield". Photograph by Fred Miller, ca. 1910.

22) Crow-Mädchen zu Pferde. Auf dem Bild ist ein Pferde-"Schild" zu sehen. Foto von Fred Miller, ca. 1910.

21) An early horse „shield", tribe unknown but probably Plateau or Crow. This dates from the 1820s and has rawhide discs some 18" (0.46 m) in diameter. It is very similar to one which was formerly in the University Museum, Cambridge, England, but is now lost. Courtesy Stoneyhurst College collection: now on loan to the Museum of Mankind, London.

21) Ein früher Pferde-"Schild", Herkunft unbekannt, aber wahrscheinlich Plateau oder Crow. Er stammt aus den 1820er Jahren und hat Rohhautscheiben von etwa 18 Zoll (0.46 m) Durchmesser. Er gleicht sehr einem Stück, das sich früher im University Museum von Cambridge, England, befand und jetzt verschwunden ist. Mit Genehmigung der Stoneyhurst College-Sammlung, jetzt als Leihgabe im Museum of Mankind, London.

23) Horse used to transport a Blackfeet Medicine Pipe Bundle. Painting by Nicolas Point, c. 1840. Note the shield-like attachment at the front of the horse. (See Point, Donnelly trans., 1967: 134).

23) Pferd zum Transport eines Blackfeet-Medizinpeifenbündels. Gemälde von Nicolas Point, ca. 1840. Man beachte die schildartige Befestigung vorn am Pferd. (Siehe Point, Donnelly trans., 1967: 134.)

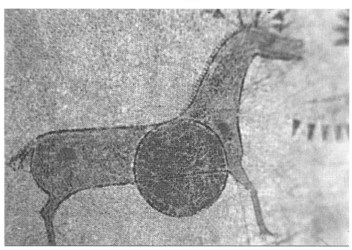

24 a) Protective shield on a horse. Pictograph by the Mandan chief, Mato-tope, 1834. (Historisches Museum, Bern, Switzerland. Specimen no. NA8). There is a shield similar to this - painted completely red and identified as Mandan - in the collections of the Museum of Mankind, London. (Specimen no. 5021). (However, it is possibly Pawnee).

24 a) Schutzschild auf einem Pferd. Piktographie von dem Mandan-Häuptling Mato-tope, 1834. (Historisches Museum, Bern, Schweiz, Exemplar Nr. NA8.) Es gibt einen Schild, der diesem ähnlich ist - vollständig rot gefärbt und als Mandan identifiziert - in den Sammlungen des Museum of Mankind, London. (Exemplar No. 5021) (Er stammt jedoch möglicherweise von den Pawnee.)

24 b) Horse „shield" designs, contrasted. Upper is now in the Carnegie Museum (Specimen no. 2418-96); lower is in the Museum für Völkerkunde, Berlin (Specimen no. IVB7779. Harvey Collection, 1905). Both are probably Crow dating from c. 1880.

24 b) Pferde-"Schild"-Muster, gegenübergestellt. Das obere Stück befindet sich heute im Carnegie Museum (Nr. 2418-96), das untere im Museum für Völkerkunde in Berlin (No. IVB7779. Harvey Collection, 1905). Beide sind wahrscheinlich Crow und stammen von ca. 1880.

Der Transport der Medizinpfeife und symbolische Pferdeausrüstungsgegenstände

Ein gängiger Brauch bei den Blackfeet war der separate Transport des hochgeschätzten Pfeifenmedizinbündels. So wurde der Überlieferung zufolge in alten Tagen ein Medizinpfeifenbündel auf dem Rücken des Besitzers getragen. Zur Zeit von Nicolas Point jedoch - etwa 1840 - wurde das Bündel auf einem besonders ausgesuchten Pferd transportiert, das von allen anderen Aufgaben befreit war, und die Frau, die das Pferd führte, war *„die am höchsten geehrte Frau des Stammes"* (Point, Donnelly trans., 1967: 134). (See also Taylor 1993: 66).

Das Pferd könnte auch stärker in den Medizinbündelkomplex miteinbezogen worden sein als allgemein anerkannt. So verweist Walter McClintocks Beschreibung der Übertragung eines Blackfeet-Medizinpfeifenbündels 1904 auf die verschiedenen Gegenstände, die mit dem Bündel übertragen wurden - etwa auf die Trachten, die vom neuen Besitzer und seiner Frau getragen wurden; sie erhielten ferner ein Pferd, das ausschließlich vom Pfeifenbesitzer geritten werden durfte (McClintock, 1923: 293).

Zusätzlich scheint es eine umfangreiche Pferdeausrüstung gegeben zu haben, die sich nicht in diesen Bündeln befand, sondern mit ihnen verbunden war, wie etwa ein Lariat, eine Peitsche, ein Sattel, Zaumzeug, Martingal und Schwanzriemen - all das gehörte vermutlich zur Ausrüstung des Pferdes für den Transport des Bündels.

Clark Wissler wies ebenfalls auf die Verpflichtungen des Biberbündels hin. Er berichtete, daß eines der Pferde in bestimmter Weise bemalt und dem Ziehen des Travois, auf dem dieses älteste aller Bündel transportiert wurde, gewidmet werden mußte. Zusätzlich mußten ein besonderes Pferd für den Erwerber und eines für seine Frau ausgewählt und bemalt werden. Diese waren dann für diesen Zweck geweiht, und jenes, das das Bündel trug, durfte niemals für den Transport frischen Fleisches benutzt werden (Wissler, 1912 (a): 174).

Seltener - aber nach meiner Überzeugung Teil der symbolischen Pferderegalia - ist die Benutzung der Schabracke, die ich hier als „Decke für den Sattel, mehr oder weniger verziert, die über den Sattel oder die Ausrüstung eines Pferdes gelegt wurde", definiere. Abb. 15 zeigt eine Skizze des Schweizer Künstlers Rudolph Kurz von einem Sioux-Pferd, die er in Fort Union im Dezember 1851 anfertigte. Beachtenswert ist, daß es sich hier ganz eindeutig nicht um eine Satteldecke handelt. Die Decke reicht über Sattel und Widerrist des Pferdes. Es gibt kurze Erwähnungen in der Literatur über den Gebrauch solch einer Schabracke durch andere Stämme. 1846 beschrieb Lewis Garrard die Insignien des Pferdes einer Cheyenne-Frau, das er im Herbst 1846 in der Umgebung von Bent's Fort sah: *„Über den Sattel war blauer Stoff gebreitet, der ihr Pferd vom Widerrist bis zum Hinterteil bedeckte, wunderschön mit vielfarbigen Perlen bearbeitet und mit Blechkügelchen versehen, die von den mit Fransen besetzten Kanten klimperten"* (Hoig, 1974: 48).

Transporting the Medicine Pipe and symbolic horse accoutrements

An established custom among the Blackfeet was the separate transportation of a highly valued Pipe Medicine Bundle. Thus, according to tradition, in ancient days a Medicine Pipe Bundle was carried on the back of its owner. However, by the time of Nicolas Point - that is circa 1840 - the Bundle was carried on a specially designated horse, which was exempt from all other use, and the woman who led the horse was „*the most honored woman of the tribe*" (Point, Donnelly trans., 1967: 134).(See also Taylor 1993: 66)

The horse may also be more keyed in with part of the Medicine Bundle complex than is generally recognized. Thus, Walter McClintock's description relating to the transfer of a Blackfeet Medicine Pipe Bundle in 1904 refers to the various accoutrements which went <u>with</u> the bundle - such as the costumes to be worn by the new owner and his wife; they were also given a horse which could only be ridden by the pipe owner (McClintock, 1923: 293).

Additionally, there seems to have been much horse equipment not <u>in</u> but associated <u>with</u> these Bundles, such as a lariat, whip, saddle, bridle, martingale and crupper - all presumably used to outfit the horse for the transportation of the Bundle itself.

Clark Wissler also referred to the Beaver Bundle obligations, reporting that one of the horses must be painted a certain way and devoted to bearing the travois for transporting this most ancient of Bundles. In addition, a special horse for the purchaser and one for his wife had to be selected and painted. These were then sacred for these purposes and the one used for the Bundle must never be used to transport fresh meat (Wissler, 1912 (a): 174).

Less common - but I am convinced part of symbolic horse regalia - is the use of the <u>caparison</u>, which I am defining here as „a cover for the saddle more or less ornamented and laid over the saddle or furniture of a horse". Fig. 15 shows a sketch of a Sioux horse by the Swiss artist, Rudolph Kurz, which he did at Fort Union in December 1851. Note that this is most definitely not a saddle blanket, the covering going over the saddle and withers of the horse. There are brief references in the literature to the use of such a caparison by other tribes. In 1846, Lewis Garrard described a Cheyenne woman's horse regalia which he saw in the vicinity of Bent's Fort in the autumn of that year: „*Over the saddle was blue cloth, beautifully worked with multicolored beads and with tin pellets that jangled from the fringed edges, which covered her horse from wethers to rump*" (Hoig, 1974: 48).

Such regalia does seem associated with women's horses - note the woman standing by in the Kurz sketch. The quilled decoration in the form of a series of horseshoes almost certainly makes reference to horses captured in warfare - a widespread symbol to convey this message. Such horseshoe symbols occur on various types of costume - on a Sioux shirt collected by Francis Parkman in 1846, on moccasins and on a Sioux woman's dress, which I refer to later.

Derartige Ausrüstungen scheinen zu den Pferden der Frauen gehört zu haben - man beachte in der Kurz-Skizze die daneben stehende Frau. Die Quillverzierung in Form einer Serie von Pferdehufen weist höchstwahrscheinlich auf Pferde hin, die im Krieg erbeutet wurden - ein weitverbreitetes Symbol zur Übermittlung dieser Botschaft. Derartige Hufsymbole erscheinen auf verschiedenen Arten von Trachten - auf einem von Francis Parkman 1846 gesammelten Sioux-Hemd, auf Mokassins und auf einem Sioux-Frauenkleid, das ich später erwähnen werde.

Pferdeschabracken oder „*Sattelhüllen*" (Ewers, 1955: 95) sind außerordentlich selten. Die einzige, die ich in den ethnographischen Sammlungen gefunden habe, wird in den Abbildungen 2 und 3 (Einführung) gezeigt und befindet sich heute im Sheffield Museum, England. Sie ist Teil der Wharncliffe-Sammlung, die vor 1873 zusammengetragen wurde. Man beachte wie bemerkenswert ähnlich sie jener ist, die Kurz darstellt - man sieht auch den leicht überdehnten, abgewetzten Teil der Haut, der offensichtlich über das Sattelhorn gezogen wurde. Hufmotive sind in Quillwork ausgeführt (Abb. 16), und anstelle von Glöckchen - wie in der Kurz-Skizze - sind Afterklauen an bequillten Riemen befestigt.

Ich überlege, ob es sich bei der Schabracke um einen Überrest der Pferdepanzerung handelt, die wir von Felszeichnungen und Beschreibungen früher Beobachter kennen und die in den alten Tagen vor der Einführung des Gewehrs, wahrscheinlich aufgrund spanischen Einflusses, benutzt wurde. Mann und Pferd wurden durch eine vielschichtige Hirschlederbedeckung zu einer Einheit (Abb. 17). In einer Beschreibung von Lewis und Clark über die Shoshone hieß es, daß „*sie eine Art Rüstung wie eine Panzerung haben, die aus vielfach gefalteten, gegerbten Antilopenhäuten hergestellt wird, zusammengesetzt mit Hilfe einer Mixtur aus Leim und Sand. Damit schützen sie ihre eigenen Körper und die ihrer Pferde, und es zeigte sich, daß diese für Pfeile undurchdringlich war*" (Lewis and Clark, Coues ed., 1893. Vol. 2: 561).

Es ist interessant festzustellen, daß die Bezeichnung „Kriegshemd" zweifellos von einem mehrschichtigen Kleidungsstück herrührt, das die Männer in der Schlacht trugen und das wahrscheinlich ähnlich wie das in Abb. 18 aussah. Es wurde schließlich durch ein einfaches - aber höchst symbolisches - Kriegshemd in historischer Zeit ersetzt. Könnte es ähnliche Parallelen zur Pferdepanzerung gegeben haben?

Beachtenswert ist, daß diese frühen Schabracken aus jeweils einer nahezu vollständigen Haut gefertigt wurden, an der sich noch die Läufe befanden. Später - und in Übereinstimmung mit Änderungen der Tracht - wurden sie durch besser zugeschnittene Stücke ersetzt, wie in der in Abb. 19 gezeigten Skizze von Amos Bad Heart Bull.

Im Zusammenhang mit Pferdepanzerungen muß ich auf ein aus doppelter Rohhaut gefertigtes schildähnliches Objekt hinweisen, das von Zeit zu Zeit in den ethnographischen Sammlungen auftaucht. Das in Abb. 20 gezeigte Stück befindet sich in der Laura Fisher-Sammlung, jenes in Abb. 21 im *Museum of Mankind*, London, England. Eine interessante Fotografie von Miller, die Anfang

Horse caparisons or „*saddle housings*" (Ewers, 1955: 95) are exceedingly rare. The only one which I have found in the ethnographical collections is shown in Figs. 2 + 3 (Introduction), and which is now in the Sheffield Museum, England. It is part of the Wharncliffe collection which was made prior to 1873. Note how remarkably similar to that shown by Kurz - you can see too the slightly stretched and worn part of the hide where it has obviously gone over the pommel of the saddle. Horseshoe motifs are in quillwork (Fig. 16) and, instead of bells as in the Kurz sketch, there are dew-claws attached to quilled thongs.

I wonder if the caparison is a remnant of the horse armor which we know from Rock Art pictures and descriptions by early observers, which was used in early days prior to the introduction of the gun, probably due to Spanish influence, both man and horse integrated by a multilayered buckskin covering (Fig. 17). One description by Lewis and Clark for the Shoshone was that „*they have a kind of armor like a coat of mail, which is formed of a great many folds of dressed antelope-skins, united by means of a mixture of glue and sand. With this they cover their own bodies and those of their horses, and find it impervious to arrows*" (Lewis and Clark, Coues ed., 1893. Vol. 2: 561).

It is of interest to note that the term warshirt undoubtedly derives from a multilayered garment worn by men in battle, which probably looked something like this. (Fig. 18) This was ultimately replaced by a single-layered - but highly symbolic - warshirt in the historic period. Could there be similar parallels with horse armor?

Note that these early caparisons were fabricated from an almost complete skin with the legs still intact. Later - and consistent with costume changes - they were replaced by a more tailored style as shown in the sketch by Amos Bad Heart Bull (Fig. 19).

While on the subject of horse armor, I should make reference to a rawhide double shield-like object which turns up from time to time in the ethnographical collections. The one shown in Fig. 20 is in the Laura Fisher collection, and the one in Fig. 21 in the Museum of Mankind, London. An interesting Miller photograph taken in the early 1900s, shows one of these in use (Fig. 22), and while both Horst Hartmann (1968) and more recently, Gaylord Torrence (1994), have described these simply as „saddle ornaments", I am inclined to think that they were somewhat more than this. Fig. 23 shows, for example, one on the Blackfeet horse which was used to transport the Medicine Bundle[5] and which was mentioned earlier; the fact that it is associated with sacred materials suggests that it might be part of the Medicine Bundle accoutrements and gives symbolic protection to the horse and its precious load. Such double shield-like devices are generally small, the shield disc seldom exceeding 14 inches (0.36 m); nevertheless, as has been well documented, it was actually the designs on the shield which were considered to give the protective power rather than the

---

[5] I am indebted to John C. Ewers for drawing my attention to this. Paul Ritner and his friend the late Tom Lindsay of Glasgow, contributed considerably to my researches on the caparison.

dieses Jahrhunderts aufgenommen wurde, zeigt eines davon im Gebrauch. (Abb.22) Sowohl Horst Hartmann als auch erst vor kurzem Gaylord Torrence beschreiben diese Objekte einfach als „Satteldekoration". Ich glaube jedoch, sie stellten etwas mehr als das dar. Abb. 23 zeigt beispielsweise eines auf einem Blackfeet-Pferd, das zum Transport des Medizinbündels benutzt und das vorher erwähnt wurde.[5] Die Tatsache, daß es mit sakralen Gegenständen in Verbindung steht, läßt vermuten, daß es Teil des Medizinbündelzubehörs sein könnte und symbolisch das Pferd und seine wertvolle Ladung schützt. Solche doppelschildartigen Objekte sind im allgemeinen klein, die Schildscheibe ist selten größer als 14 Inch im Durchmesser; nichts destoweniger waren es, wie gut dokumentiert ist, tatsächlich mehr die Muster auf dem Schild, die als schützende Kraft angesehen wurden, als der materielle Schutz durch die Rohhaut. Einige Beweise lassen jedoch vermuten, daß sie tatsächlich, wie die großen Schilde der Krieger zu Fuß, in alten Tagen als mechanischer Schutz gegen Pfeile, Lanzen oder Musketenkugeln dienten. So hat das Stück in Abb. 21 - vielleicht das älteste noch existierende, das in die 1820er Jahre datiert - große Scheiben von etwa 18 Inches im Durchmesser, und ein ähnliches Stück (Abb. 24 a) scheint von *Mato-tope*, dem Mandan-Häuptling, auf eine Robe gemalt worden zu sein, die heute im Historischen Museum in Bern, in der Schweiz, liegt. Dieser Schild bedeckte die Rippen des Pferdes, einen der verletzlichsten Teile des Körpers.

Es scheint mir, daß im Verlauf der Zeit und mit der Einführung stärkerer Gewehre die Betonung jetzt auf dem symbolischen Schutz lag, der durch die gemalten Muster gewährleistet wurde, und der Schild wurde verkleinert. Weil er am Sattel befestigt war, hatte der Reiter die Hände frei, seine Waffen optimal zu benutzen.

Insbesondere auf den späteren „Schilden" sind diese Muster bemerkenswert ähnlich ... stets geometrisch und bestehend aus Scheiben und dreieckigen Dekors, manchmal mit einem Morgensternmotiv (mit dem, nebenbei, eine Art Schutzsymbolismus verbunden war). (Abb. 24 b) Bill Holm hat mir gegenüber kürzlich geäußert, daß einige der Designs interessante Parallelen aufweisen. Er glaubte, daß dies sehr bedeutsam war, weil *„es nicht selbstverständlich für einen Maler ist, so etwas zu tun"* (B. Holm an C. F. T., 2. September 1994).[6]

---

[5] Ich stehe in John C. Ewers Schuld, daß er meine Aufmerksamkeit darauf gelenkt hat. Paul Ritner und sein Freund, der verstorbene Tom Lindsay aus Glasgow trugen bemerkenswert zu meinen Recherchen über die Schabracke bei.

[6] Bill Holm stellte die folgenden Überlegungen über diese interessanten Pferdeschilde an, die hier wiedergegeben werden müssen: *„Alle Exemplare, von denen ich über Bilder verfüge, weisen sehr interessante Ähnlichkeiten auf. Beispielsweise haben sie eine gerade Linie mit unterschiedlichen Details und Farben, die quer über den oberen Rand des runden Musters gezogen sind. Das scheint mir sehr bedeutsam, da es sicherlich nicht üblich für einen Maler ist, so etwas zu tun. Wie erwähnt, ist das Spalding-Set noch immer am Sattel befestigt, und die Zaumzeugriemen passen exakt durch die Öffnungen in der Mitte beider Schürzen. Ich habe das Buch von Fred Miller nicht zur Hand ..., daher kann ich dieses Set nicht mit dem anderen vergleichen, aber so wie ich die Bilder in Erinnerung habe, erscheint es in derselben Position*

mechanical protection of the rawhide. However, there is some evidence which suggests that, as with the large shields of pedestrian warriors, in early days they did serve as a mechanical protection against arrows and lances or musket-loading guns. Thus, the specimen in Fig. 21 - probably the earliest in existence and dating from the 1820s - has large discs some 18 inches (0.46 m) in diameter and a similar device (Fig. 24 a) seems to have been depicted by *Mato-tope*, the Mandan chief, on a robe now in the Historisches Museum, Bern, Switzerland. This shield covers the horse's ribs - one of the most vulnerable parts of the body.

It seems to me that with the progress of time, and with the introduction of high-powered rifles, the emphasis was now on the symbolic protection afforded by the painted designs, and the shield was reduced in size. By being attached to the saddle, it left the hands free enabling the rider to maximize the use of his weapons.

On the later „shields" in particular, these designs are remarkably similar ... always geometrical and consisting of discs and triangular patterns sometimes with a Morning Star motif (which, incidentally, had protective-type symbolism associated with it) (Fig. 24 b). Bill Holm has recently commented to me that some of the designs have interesting similarities. He felt that this was very significant as it „*isn't a natural thing for a painter to do*" (B. Holm to C. F. T., Sept. 2, 1994).[6]

auf dem Pferd wie bei dem Spalding-Sattel. Entsprechend der Herkunft des Sattels und der dazugehörigen Schürzen und dem Schwanzriemen scheint es sicher ein Spalding-Stück zu sein. Da nichts sonst in der Sammlung aussieht, als stamme es von den Crow, gibt es, außer seiner Ähnlichkeit zu späteren Crow-Stücken, keinen Grund zu der Annahme, daß es von den Crow hergestellt wurde... Ich würde für einen Crow-Ursprung plädieren, wenn es einen recht guten Beweis gäbe, aber ich bin geneigt, einen Nez Perce-Ursprung anzunehmen, bis bessere Informationen verfügbar sind. Ich neige zu dieser Annahme, daß, obwohl es als Schutzschild gegen Abschürfungen durch Gepäck gedient haben könnte, die schlagenden Ähnlichkeiten der ungewöhnlichen Muster auf jedem Teil trotz des großen zeitlichen Abstands (und vielleicht auch der räumlichen Distanz) eine Art symbolischen oder zeremoniellen Zweck nahelegen. In der Plazierung ähneln sie den Seitenteilen von euro-amerikanischen Sätteln, und vielleicht wurden sie von diesen beeinflußt" (Brief von Bill Holm an C. F. Taylor, September 1994).

[6] Bill Holm makes the following observations on these interesting horse shields which should be recorded: „*All of the ones I have pictures of have very interesting similarities. For example they have a straight line with varying details and color cutting right across the upper edge of the circular design. This seems to me to be very significant, as it certainly isn't a natural thing for a painter to do. As I mentioned, the Spalding set is still attached to the saddle and the rigging passes right through the holes in the centers of the two skirts. I don't have the Fred Miller book handy ... so I can't compare that set with the others, but as I remember the pictures, it appears on the horse in the same position as it would with the Spalding saddle. As to the origin of that saddle and associated skirts and crupper, it seems to surely be a Spalding piece. Since nothing else in the collection looks Crow there is no reason except its similarity to later Crow pieces to assume it was Crow made... I would argue a Crow origin if there was pretty good proof, but I'm inclined to believe a Nez Perce origin until better information comes along. As to function, I'm inclined to the idea that, although it could work as a protective shield against pack abrasion, the striking similarity of the unusual designs on each of these, even though widely separated in time (and perhaps place), suggests some kind of symbolic or ceremonial use. In placement it resembles the skirts of Euro-American saddles, and maybe owes something to them.*" (Letter Bill Holmes to C. F. T., September 1994).

25 a) Mask on Nez Perce horse, photograph by Lee Moorhouse in 1906. Horse masks were early used by Plains (and probably Plateau) tribes. The explorer, Alexander Henry, describes them for the Cheyenne, in 1806 (see text).

25 a) Masken auf Nez Perce-Pferden, fotografiert von Lee Moorhouse, 1906. Pferdemasken wurden früh von Plains- (und wahrscheinlich Plateau-)Stämmen benutzt. Der Entdecker Alexander Henry beschreibt sie 1806 für die Cheyenne. (Siehe Text.)

25 b) Horse mask sketch by the Blackfeet warrior, Red Plume. Wissler refers to these coverings as „horse bonnets" and reported that one side was always painted red and the other blue (See horse altar, Fig. 12; also Wissler, 1913: 457). Note the horns attached to this mask which probably evoke buffalo power.

25 b) Skizze einer Pferdemaske von dem Blackfeetkrieger Red Plume. Wissler bezeichnete diese Bedeckung als „Pferdehauben" und berichtete, das immer eine Seite rot und die andere blau gefärbt war. (Siehe Pferdealtar, Abb. 12; auch Wissler, 1913: 457). Man beachte die an der Maske befestigten Hörner, wahrscheinlich zur Beschwörung von Büffelkraft.

26) A buffalo-horse rawhide cut-out, Crow, c. 1870, collected by William Wildschut about 1915. It is suggested that this rawhide cut-out was made for a War or Horse Capture Bundle (See Maurer et al. 1992: 149).

26) Ein aus Rohhaut geschnittenes Büffel-Pferd, Crow, ca. 1870, gesammelt von William Wildschut um 1915. Es wird angenommen, daß dieser Rohhautausschnitt für ein Kriegs- oder Pferderaubbündel angefertigt wurde. (Siehe Maurer et al. 1992: 149.)

27 and 28) Buffalo and horse power combined. Sioux Horse Dreamers Society. The lower figure is by the artist, Kills Two, and refers to the origin tale of the Society (See text). (Original is in the Yale University Library).

27 und 28) Kombinierte Bison- und Pferdekraft. Horse Dreamers-Gesellschaft der Sioux. Die untere Abbildung stammt von dem Künstler Kills Two und bezieht sich auf die Ursprungsgeschichte der Gesellschaft. (Siehe Text.) Original in der Yale University Library.

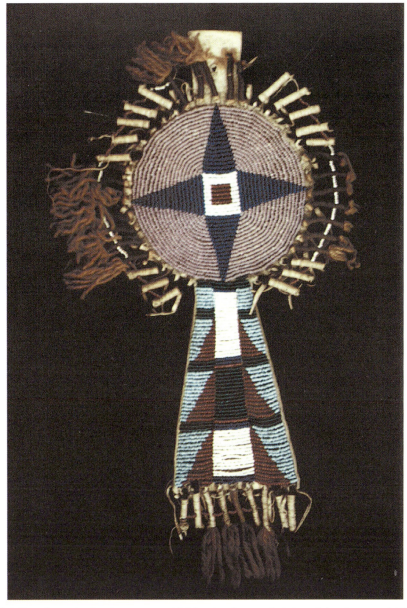

29) A Crow horse forehead ornament with Morning Star symbol. An origin of a powerful War Medicine Bundle which originally belonged to the warrior, Blows Down, it refers to a gift from the Morning Star which gave help and success in warfare (C. F. Taylor collection, Hastings). (See Wildschut, Ewers ed., 1960: 45).

29) Stirnornament eines Crow-Pferdes mit Morgensternsymbol. Es stammt aus dem mächtigen Kriegsmedizinbündel, das ursprünglich dem Krieger Blows Down gehörte. Es bezieht sich auf ein Geschenk des Morgensterns, der Hilfe und Erfolg im Krieg verlieh. (C. F. Taylor-Sammlung, Hastings) (Siehe Wildschut, Ewers ed., 1960: 45.)

30) Scalp on bridle. Sioux beadwork figure, c. 1880. It has been reported (Vestal, 1934: 187) that such ornaments symbolically stated that the owner had ridden down the enemy. (C. F. Taylor collection, Hastings).

30) Skalp an Zaumzeug. Sioux-Perlenarbeit, ca. 1880. Es wurde berichtet (Vestal, 1934: 187), solcher Schmuck sage symbolisch aus, daß der Besitzer den Feind niedergeritten hatte. (C. F. Taylor-Sammlung, Hastings)

31) Horse tail with symbolic Thunderbird embellishment. (Musee de l'Homme, Paris. Specimen no. MH86.17.1). This probably dates from at least 1840. Photograph by C. F. Taylor.

31) Pferdeschweif mit symbolischer Donnervogeldekoration. (Musee de l'Homme, Paris. Nr. MH86.17.1) Wahrscheinlich mindestens aus der Zeit um 1840. Foto von C. F. Taylor.

32 a) Eagle feathers tied in the horse's tail - generally interpreted as symbolic of thunder power. Sketch by Amos Bad Heart Bull. (See Blish, 1967: 202).

32 a) In den Pferdeschweif gebundene Adlerfeder - im allgemeinen als Symbol für die Macht des Donnervogels interpretiert. Skizze von Amos Bad Heart Bull. (Siehe Blish, 1967: 202.)

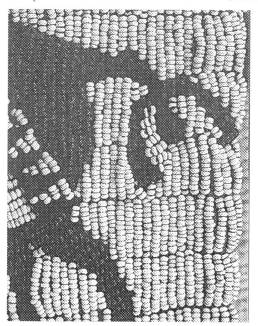

32 b) Red cloth tie on a horse's tail. Sioux beaded figure, c. 1880. According to Dr. J. R. Walker, this was indicative among the Sioux of a war horse (See Walker, DeMallie and Jahner eds., 1980: 278). (C. F. Taylor collection, Hastings).

32 b) Rote Stoffschleife an Pferdeschweif. Sioux-Perlenarbeit, ca. 1880. Dr. J. R. Walker zufolge wies dies unter den Sioux auf ein Kriegspferd hin. (Siehe Walker, DeMallie und Jahner eds., 1980: 278.) (C. F. Taylor-Sammlung, Hastings)

33) War bridle and head-dress used by the Crow chief Sees-the-Living-Bull. The split owl feather head-dress was said to help the horse see at night. The black feathers on the bridle were said to symbolize birds (ravens?) circling their prey and the red cloth symbolizes lightning. Sees-the-Living-Bull was said to have lightning power. (Photograph and data courtesy Richard Edwards, Toledo, Ohio.).

33) Kriegszaumzeug und Kopfschmuck, benutzt von dem Crow Chief Sees-the-Living-Bull. Der Kopfschmuck aus gespleißten Eulenfedern sollte dem Pferd, wie gesagt wurde, helfen, bei Nacht zu sehen. Es hieß, daß die schwarzen Federn am Zaumzeug Vögel (Raben?), die ihre Beute umkreisen, symbolisieren, und der rote Stoff stellt den Blitz dar. Man sagte, daß Sees-the-Living-Bull über die Kraft des Blitzes verfügte. (Foto und Angaben genehmigt von Richard Edwards, Toledo, Ohio.)

34) Running off horses, „a robust, manly pastime" (Smith, 1943: 93). Sketch is by His Fight or *O-ki-tcin Ta'-wa* („Jaw"), Hunkpapa Sioux, c. 1880.

34) Pferderaub, „ein rauher, männlicher Zeitvertreib" (Smith, 1943: 93), Skizze von His Fight oder *O-ki-tcin Ta'-wa* („Jaw"), Hunkpapa Sioux, ca. 1880.

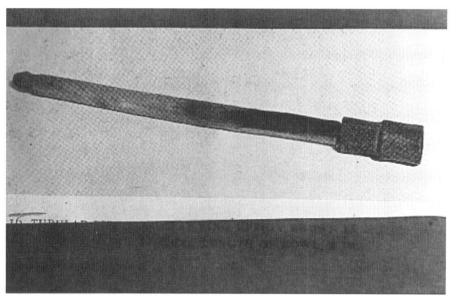

35) A typical early style of War Pipe where the bowl was in direct line with the stem. (See Wildschut, Ewers ed., 1960: Fig. 16).

35) Typische frühe Art der Kriegspfeife, bei der der Kopf sich in direkter Linie mit dem Pfeifenstiel befand. (Siehe Wildschut, Ewers ed., 1960: Abb. 16.)

Masken, Kopfschmuck und Kriegsbündel

Kaum umstritten ist der Gebrauch von Pferdemasken, der auf spanischen Einfluß zurückgehen könnte, aber derartige Ausrüstungsstücke waren tatsächlich weit verbreitet - Abb. 25 a zeigt eine Maske aus der Plateau-Region - und wurden in alten Zeiten benutzt. Als der Entdecker Alexander Henry 1806 eine Hidatsa-Handelsgruppe zu einem Cheyennedorf begleitete, ritten ihnen einige Cheyenne auf schönen Pferden entgegen, die *„in höchst sonderbarer Weise maskiert waren, um den Kopf eines Büffels, eines Rothirsches, oder eines Cabrie mit Hörnern zu imitieren. Maul und Nüstern - sogar die Augen - waren von rotem Stoff umrandet"* (Henry und Thompson, Coues ed., 1897. Vol. I: 377). Möglicherweise legten die Cheyenne besonderen Wert auf solche Pferdemasken - sicher stammt eine der schönsten in den Sammlungen von diesem Stamm -, obwohl John Ewers berichtete, 1942 ähnliches bei den Blackfeet gesehen zu haben (Ewers, 1955: 100), und Bradley beschrieb 1882 eine Maske der Blackfeet, die *„aus dem Kopf eines Büffels hergestellt war, mit daran befestigten Hörnern, die Augen des Pferdes sind durch die ursprünglichen Augenhöhlen in der Haut zu sehen"* (Bradley, 1923: 263).

Wie Brasser feststellt, wurde geglaubt, daß Pferdemasken für Erfolg auf dem Kriegspfad beitrugen, und jene, die von den Plains Cree benutzt wurden, zeigten manchmal *„Blitze symbolisierende Zickzacklinien, die sich von den Augenhöhlen hinunterzogen und das Weiterleben des Mississippischen Tränenden-Auge-Motivs und seine Verbindung mit dem Geist des Donners vermuten lassen"* (Brasser, 1987: 118).[7]

Unter dem wertvollen Besitz Old Suns, eines Häuptlings der nördlichen Blackfeet, befand sich eine *„sehr aufwendige Kopfbedeckung für ein Pferd, die getragen wurde, wenn es in die Schlacht ging. Ein Teil davon bedeckte den Kopf wie eine Maske, Öffnungen waren für die Augen belassen, und die Maske war mit einem Paar Hörner ausgestattet. Der andere Teil war eine Art Banner, das zum Unterkiefer hinunterhing. Beide Teile waren reichlich mit roten, gelben und blauen Federn dekoriert"* (Ewers, 1955: 99-100). Wissler erhielt einige Blackfeet-Skizzen von solchen Ausrüstungsstücken (Abb. 25 b), und obwohl zu dieser Zeit nichts über den Symbolismus erklärt wurde, haben wir hier sicherlich eine symbolische Kombination von Pferde- und Büffel-Kraft, während die Pferdehalsbänder von Pferdemedizinmännern gemacht und gesegnet wurden, um die Reiter in der Schlacht zu schützen. Derartige Vorstellungen werden in ähnlicher Weise bei den Crow (Wildschut, Ewers ed., 1960: 52) und den Sioux ausgedrückt. (Densmore 1918:388-9)[8]

Abb. 26 zeigt beispielsweise (Maurer et al., 1992: 149) einen Rohhautzuschnitt der Crow, der von William Wildschut gesammelt wurde, er datiert von etwa 1870. Hier steht der Erfolg im Krieg in engem Zusammenhang mit dem

---

[7] „Macloed (Alberta) Advance", 26. Mai 1908. Ein Artikel mit dem Titel „An Indian Parade" von F. W. Maunsell. (Brief von Hugh Dempsey an C. F. T., 28. 6. 1994.)

[8] Siehe auch Fußnote 9.

Masks, Head Ornaments and War Bundles

Less contentious is the use of horse masks, which may have been a Spanish influence, but such accoutrements did have wide distribution - Fig. 25 a shows one used on the Plateau - and they were anciently used. Thus, in 1806, when the explorer Alexander Henry, accompanied a Hidatsa trading party to a Cheyenne village, some of the Cheyenne rode out to meet them on fine horses which *„were masked in a very singular manner, to imitate the head of a buffalo, red deer, or cabbrie with horns, the mouth and nostrils - even the eyes - trimmed with red cloth"* (Henry and Thompson, Coues ed., 1897. Vol. I: 377). Possibly, the Cheyenne put emphasis on such horse masks - certainly, one of the finest in the collections comes from that tribe - although John Ewers did report on seeing something similar from the Blackfeet in 1942 (Ewers, 1955: 100), and Bradley, in 1882, described one for the Blackfeet as *„made of the head of the buffalo, the horns attached, the eyes of the horse appearing through the original eye holes of the skin"* (Bradley, 1923: 263).

As Brasser observes, horse masks were believed to convey success in warfare and those used by the Plains Cree sometimes exhibited *„lightning symbols zigzagging down from the eyeholes suggesting the survival of the Mississippian weeping-eye motif and its association with the thunder spirit"* (Brasser, 1987: 118).[7]

Among the valued possessions of Old Sun, a North Blackfeet chief, was a *„very elaborate headgear for a horse to wear when going into battle. One part of it covered the head like a mask, holes being left for the eyes, and was fitted with a pair of horns; the other part was a sort of banner, to be suspended to the lower jaw; both parts were profusely decorated with red, yellow, and blue feathers"* (Ewers, 1955: 99-100). Wissler obtained some Blackfeet sketches (Fig. 25 b) of such accoutrements and although the symbolism was not given at the time, we surely have here a symbolic combination of horse and buffalo power while the horse collars were made by Horse Medicine Men and blessed to give protection to their riders in battle. Such ideas find similar expressions among both the Crow (Wildschut, Ewers, ed., 1960: 52) and Sioux. (Densmore, 1918:388-9)[8]

Fig. 26, for example, shows (Maurer et al., 1992: 149) a Crow rawhide cut-out which was collected by William Wildschut and dates from about 1870. Here the success in war is closely associated with the acquisition of power through spiritual assistance, the cut-out being made for a War or Horse Capture Bundle; it shows a combination of the body of a horse with the feet, horns, and protruding tongue of the bull buffalo. Note also the image painted on a Lakota shield (Fig. 27), which shows head covering remarkably similar to the Blackfeet horse mask which I mentioned previously. Again, we have a combination of horse and buffalo, the spiritual nature of the animal and its association with thunder power being indicated by the hail and zigzag lines and the sacred

---

[7] „Macleod (Alberta) Advance". May 26, 1908. Article entitled „An Indian Parade" by F. W. Maunsell. (Letter Hugh Dempsey to C. F. T. 28. 6. 1994).

[8] See also footnote 9.

Erwerb von Kraft durch spirituelle Hilfe. Der Zuschnitt wurde für ein Kriegsoder Pferderaubbündel hergestellt; er zeigt eine Kombination aus einem Pferdekörper mit den Füßen, den Hörnern und der herausgestreckten Zunge des Bisonbullen. Beachtenswert ist ebenfalls das auf ein Lakota-Schild gemaltes Bild (Abb. 27), das eine Kopfbedeckung zeigt, die der Blackfeet-Pferdemaske, die ich vorher erwähnt habe, bemerkenswert ähnlich ist. Wieder haben wir eine Mischung aus Pferd und Bison. Der spirituelle Charakter des Tieres und seine Verbindung mit der Kraft des Donners werden von Hagel und Zickzack-Linien und dem Symbol des Heiligen Reifens angedeutet. Diese besondere Schildbemalung kann mit ziemlicher Sicherheit mit der Horse Dreamers' Society (Abb. 28) in Verbindung gebracht werden, deren Ursprungsgeschichte sich auf ein Donnerpferd bezieht, das sich durch einen schweren Sturm mit Donner, Blitz und Regen zum Himmel erhebt (ibid., und Wissler, 1912 (b): 95-98).

Himmlische Kräfte scheinen mit diesem Schlüssellochornament (Abb. 29), das bei den Crow in der zweiten Hälfte des 19. Jahrhunderts so populär war, verbunden gewesen zu sein. Die meisten waren mit dem höchst symbolischen Morgensternemblem verziert. So bezieht sich die Ursprungsmythe eines sehr machtvollen Kriegsmedizinbündels der Crow auf ein Geschenk des Morgensterns. Es befähigte den Besitzer, den Feind zu lokalisieren und seine Stärke einzuschätzen. Dies paßt gut zu seiner Verwendung zusammen mit Crow-Pferdeinsignien, wie sie in Reiterparaden benutzt wurden, bei denen es nicht unüblich für eine Frau war, die sakrale und militärische Ausrüstung ihres Mannes zu zeigen.

Normalerweise wurde auch zusätzlich ein Skalp gezeigt, der vom Zaumzeug des Pferdes hing (Abb. 30), vermutlich eine Anregung, die von dem beliebten und weitverbreiteten spanischen *Cheleno*-Zaumzeug herrührte, das aus einer metallenen Gebißstange und langen, eisernen oder kupfernen Kettengliedern darunter bestand, die - wie Boller sagte - „*bei der kleinsten Bewegung des Pferdes klirrten*" (Boller, 1868: 65). Der hängende Skalp jedoch war mehr als nur Schmuck. Vestal berichtete für die Sioux, daß nur Pferde, mit denen ein Feind niedergeritten worden war, einen solchen Schmuck tragen durften (Vestal, 1934:187).

Auch die Schweife der Pferde waren geschmückt, ein Charakteristikum von offensichtlich beachtlichem Alter. So sind auf einer frühen Robe im *Musée de l'Homme* in Paris mehrere Pferde mit einem donnervogelähnlichen Motiv in ihrem Schweif abgebildet, wie jenes in Abb. 31. Symbolisch nicht weit entfernt ist die realistischere Darstellung von Adlerfedern - oft ein Symbol der Kraft des Donners - die am Schweif befestigt sind.[9] (Abb. 32 a)

---

[9] Pferdeschweife, an denen roter Stoff befestigt ist, kennzeichnen im Symbolismus der Sioux ein Kriegspferd, das sich auf dem Schlachtfeld besonders ausgezeichnet hatte. So erklärte Teal Duck (*Siyaka*), daß er, als er auf dem Schlachtfeld in Bedrängnis geriet, absaß, vor seinem Pferd stand und zu ihm sprach:"*Wir sind in Gefahr. Folge mir ohne zu zögern, so daß wir siegen werden. Wenn du um dein und mein Leben läufst, tu dein Bestes, und wenn wir wieder daheim sind, werde ich dir die beste Adlerfeder geben, die ich bekommen kann, und die schönste sina'lu'ta, und du sollst mit den besten Farben bemalt werden*" (Densmore, 1918: 298). N. B. „*Die Adlerfeder war am Pferdeschweif festgebunden, und die sina'lu'ta war ein Streifen roten Stoffs, der um den Hals des Pferdes gelegt wurde*" (ibid.)

hoop symbol. This particular shield image can be rather firmly keyed in with the Horse Dreamers' Society (Fig. 28) whose origin tale refers to a thunder horse rising through a great storm of thunder, lightning and rain to reach the heavens (ibid. and Wissler, 1912 (b): 95-98).

Sky powers seem to be associated with this keyhole-shaped ornament (Fig. 29) which was so popular with the Crow in the latter half of the nineteenth century. Most of them were decorated with a Morning Star emblem which was highly symbolic. Thus, the origin myth of a very powerful War Medicine Bundle from the Crow refers to a gift from the Morning Star which enabled the owner to both locate and assess the strength of the enemy. All this ties in well with its employment on Crow horse regalia used in mounted parades, when it was not uncommon for the woman to display her husband's sacred and military paraphernalia.

Commonly displayed too, was the addition of a scalp hanging from the bridle of the horse (Fig. 30), an idea perhaps derived from the popular and widespread Spanish *chelleno* bridle which consisted of a metal bit and long iron or copper links below, which as Boller said „*jingled with the slightest movement of the horse*" (Boller, 1868: 65). The scalp drop, however, became more than a mere ornament; Vestal reported for the Sioux that only horses which had been used to ride down an enemy could use such an ornament (Vestal, 1934: 187).

The tails of horses were also embellished, a feature which is obviously of considerably antiquity. Thus, on an early robe in the *Musée de l'Homme* in Paris, there are several horses depicted with a Thunderbird-like motif within the tail such as that shown in Fig. 31; not far removed symbolically is this more realistic rendering where eagle feathers - often a symbol of thunder power - are attached to the tail.[9] (Fig. 32 a)

On other occasions, the feathers were dispensed with and instead a red cloth tie was used (Fig. 32 b); this - according to Walker - was indicative, among the Sioux, of a war-horse (Walker, DeMallie and Jahner eds., 1980: 278), while a tied tail, according to the Crow, enabled them to run faster (Ewers, 1955: 101). Later, in less stressful times, some women were surprisingly patriotic - feathers or other embellishments being replaced by an American flag!

War bridles were also widely used. Such objects were actually described by Clark Wissler for the Blood as „*a thing to tie on the halter*" (Wissler, 1912 (a): 107). John Ewers informs me that in 1941, when on the Blackfeet Reservation in Montana, he saw such a bridle still in use by an owner of horse medicine which may now be the example later acquired by the Glenbow Foundation in

---

[9] Horses' tails tied with a red cloth signified in Sioux symbolism a war-horse which had particularly distinguished itself on the battlefield. Thus, Teal Duck (*Siyaka*) explained that on one occasion when he was hard pressed on the battlefield, he dismounted and stood in front of his horse, spoke to him, saying „*We are in danger. Obey me prompt that we may conquer. If you have to run for your life and mine, do your best, and if we reach home I will give you the best eagle feather I can get and the finest sina'lu'ta, and you shall be painted with the best paint*" (Densmore, 1918: 298). N. B. „The eagle feather was tied to the horse's tail, and the sina'lu'ta was a strip of red cloth fastened around the horse's neck" (ibid.).

Bei anderen Gelegenheiten wurde auf Federn verzichtet, statt dessen wurde ein rotes Band benutzt (Abb. 32 b); dieses Band kennzeichnete - Walker zufolge - bei den Sioux ein Kriegspferd (Walker, DeMallie and Jahner eds., 1980: 278), während ein verknoteter Schweif, den Crow zufolge, die Pferde befähigte, schneller zu laufen (Ewers, 1955: 101). Später, in weniger aufregenden Zeiten, zeigten sich einige Frauen überraschend patriotisch - Federn oder anderer Schmuck wurden durch eine amerikanische Fahne ersetzt!

Kriegszaumzeug wurde ebenfalls weithin benutzt. Derartige Objekte wurden in der Tat von Clark Wissler für die Blood als „*eine Sache zur Befestigung am Halfter*" beschrieben (Wissler 1912 (a): 107). John Ewers berichtete mir, daß er 1941, als er sich auf der Blackfeet-Reservation in Montana aufhielt, solch ein Zaumzeug bei dem Besitzer einer Pferdemedizin noch immer im Gebrauch sah. Es könnte sich heute um das Stück handeln, das später von der Glenbow Foundation in Calgary, Alberta, erworben wurde. Wissler berichtete, daß über solche Objekte gesagt wurde, sie würden „*Schutz und Kraft gegen Feinde oder den Bison verleihen, indem sie die Trittsicherheit und Schnelligkeit des Pferdes erhöhten*"[10] (ibid.).

Nahezu identische Überlegungen fanden sich bei den Crow. Ein Kriegsmedizinbündel, das dem River Crow-Häuptling Two Leggings gehörte und von dem es hieß, es sei ein Geschenk des Donnervogels, enthielt eine Federkette, die um den Hals des Pferdes gelegt wurde. Durch ihre Kraft, so wurde berichtet, „*fühlte sich das Pferd so leicht wie eine Feder und war daher imstande, schneller und leichter zu laufen*" (Wildschut, Ewers ed., 1960: 52). Fast identischer Symbolismus war auch mit der gefiederten Pferdeausrüstung verbunden, die von „Sees-the-Living-Bull" benutzt wurde (Abb. 33) (R. Edwards, Diskussion 1. September 1994).

---

[10] Song, Wissler, 1912 (a): 108.

Calgary, Alberta. Such objects, Wissler reported, were said to give „*protection and power against the enemy or buffalo in that it increases the sure-footedness and speed of the horse*"[10] (ibid.).

Almost identical sentiments were expressed by the Crow. A War Medicine Bundle - owned by Two-Leggings, a River Crow chief and said to have been a gift from the Thunderbird - contained a feather necklace for tying around the horse's neck; by its power it was reported „*the horse may feel as light as a feather and therefore be able to run faster and easier*" (Wildschut, Ewers ed., 1960: 52), and almost identical symbolism was also associated with the feathered horse accoutrements used by Sees-the-Living-Bull (Fig. 33), (R. Edwards, discussion, 1 Sept. 1994).

---

[10] Song, Wissler, 1912 (a): 108.

36 - 39) Blackfeet methods of recording the capture or horses. Note how the steps change between a full pictured form (Fig. 36) to a conventionalized bare symbol (Fig. 39). Sketches by a Piegan who was considered an authority on heraldry (See Wissler, 1911: 41).

36 - 39) Methoden der Blackfeet, die Erbeutung von Pferden zu dokumentieren. Man beachte wie die Darstellungen zwischen dem vollständigen Bild (Abb. 36) zu einem stilisierten reinen Symbol (Abb. 39) wechseln. Skizzen eines Piegan, der als Autorität für Heraldik anerkannt war. (Siehe Wissler, 1911: 41.)

40) Deaf Bull, a Crow chief. The artist, DeCost Smith, reported that the colored horsehair fringes „probably stood for horses captured in war" (Smith, 1943: 140).

40) Deaf Bull, ein Crow-Häuptling. Der Künstler DeCost Smith berichtete, daß die farbigen Pferdehaarfransen „wahrscheinlich für im Krieg erbeutete Pferde standen" (Smith, 1943: 140).

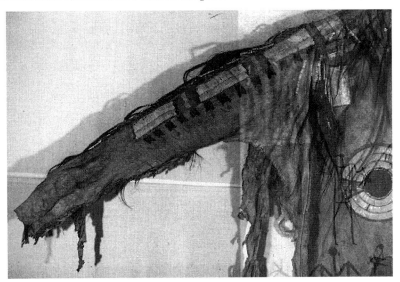

41) Detail of a quilled and fringed shirt collected by Count d'Otrante, a French nobleman, in 1842-43. He reported that its Blackfeet owner said that the horsehair locks represented horses captured. (Specimen now in the Etnografiska Museum, Stockholm. No. 1854.2.1).

41) Detail eines mit Quills und Fransen versehenen Hemdes, das von dem französischen Adligen Count d'Otrante 1842-43 gesammelt wurde. Er berichtete, daß sein Blackfeet-Besitzer sagte, die Pferdehaarsträhnen stellten erbeutete Pferde dar. (Etnografiska Museum, Stockholm. Nr. 1854.2.1)

42) A Sioux hair-fringed shirt collected by Francis Parkman at Fort Laramie in 1846. The decorations - painting and horsehair fringe - put great emphasis on horse symbolism and may actually designate a particularly successful horse raider, although this has gone unrecorded. (Specimen now at the Peabody Museum of Archaeology and Ethnology, Harvard University, No. 11004).

42) Ein Sioux-Hemd mit Haarfransen, gesammelt von Francis Parkman in Fort Laramie 1846. Die Verzierungen - Bemalungen und Pferdehaarfransen - stellen eine starke Betonung des Pferdesymbolismus dar und könnten tatsächlich einen besonders erfolgreichen Pferderäuber kennzeichnen, aber dies ist nicht dokumentiert. (Peabody Museum of Archaeology and Ethnology, Harvard University, No. 11004)

43) A magnificent Sioux hair-fringed shirt worn by Red Cloud and other dignitaries when visiting Washington in the 1870s. In addition to some two hundred and thirty-eight human hair locks, there are some sixty-eight horsehair locks - probably representing pledges of allegiance (Plains Indian Museum, Cody, Wyoming).

43) Ein prachtvolles Sioux-Hemd mit Haarfransen, das von Red Cloud und anderen Würdenträgern getragen wurde, als sie in den 1870er Jahren Washington besuchten. Zusätzlich zu etwa 238 menschlichen Haarsträhnen, weist es etwa 68 Pferdehaarsträhnen auf - wahrscheinlich repräsentierten sie Treuegelöbnisse. (Plains Indian Museum, Cody, Wyoming)

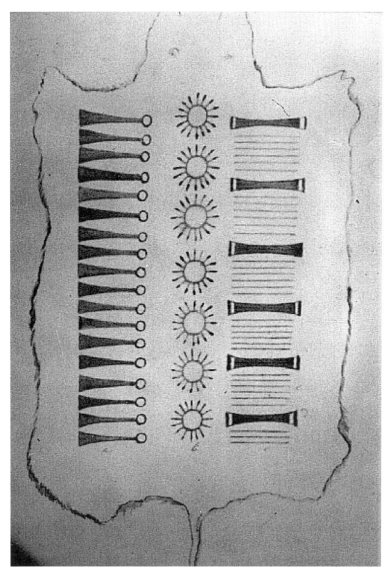

44) Copy of a robe painted by the Hidatsa chief, Yellow Bear. This was seen by Maximilian in November 1833, who reported that the symbols referred to „treasures given away" (Maximilian, 1839-41. Vol. II: 268). Note the eighteen quirts referring to the eighteen horses given - such generosity increased a man's standing. (Picture, courtesy Joslyn Art Museum, Omaha, Nebraska. Specimen no. PM8).

44) Kopie einer Robe, die von dem Hidatsa-Häuptling Yellow Bear bemalt wurde. Maximilian sah sie im November 1833. Er berichtete, daß die Symbole sich auf das „Verschenken von Wertgegenständen" bezogen. (Maximilian, 1839-41, Vol. II: 268.) Man beachte die achtzehn Reitpeitschen, die auf achtzehn verschenkte Pferde hinweisen - derartige Großzügigkeit erhöhte die Stellung eines Mannes. (Bild mit Genehmigung des Joslyn Art Museum, Omaha, Nebraska, Nr. PM8.)

45) An Oglala medicine woman wearing a dress commemorating her younger brother's horse capturing episodes against the Crow. (Photograph by Weygold, 1909. See Haberland, 1986: 85).

45) Oglala-Medizinfrau, die ein Kleid trägt, das daran erinnert, wie ihr jüngerer Bruder Pferde von den Crow erbeutete. (Foto von Weygold, 1909. Siehe Haberland, 1986: 85.)

46) A magnificent buffalo robe, Sioux or Cheyenne (?), dating from circa 1840. Note the various colored horses - red, blue/green, yellow; the colors could be symbolically significant. (Deutsches Ledermuseum, Offenbach. Specimen no. 5772). Of further interest is that the paintings are very similar to those on the Sioux (?) shirt now in the Musee de l'Homme, Paris (Specimen no. 09-19-57). (See Taylor, 1975: 48).

46) Eine prächtige Bisonrobe, Sioux oder Cheyenne (?), von ca. 1840. Man beachte die verschiedenfarbigen Pferde - rot, blau-grün, gelb. Die Farben könnten symbolisch bedeutsam sein. (Deutsches Ledermuseum, Offenbach. Nr. 5772) Von weiterem Interesse ist, daß die Bemalungen jenen auf dem Sioux-Hemd (?) sehr gleichen, das sich heute im Musee l'Homme, Paris, befindet (Nr. 09-19-57). (Siehe Taylor, 1975: 48.)

Das Erbeuten von Pferden

Wie DeCost Smith feststellte, war das Wegtreiben von Pferden des Feindes sowohl legitim als auch ehrenhaft (Abb. 34): *„Als Aggressions- oder Vergeltungsmaßnahme hatte es doppelte Wirkung: es bereicherte den Plünderer, während es dem Geplünderten den Besitz entzog, der unentbehrlich für seine Sicherheit und sein Wohlergehen war. Als robuster, männlicher Zeitvertreib war es ferner eine glänzende Übung in den spartanischen Tugenden - Geduld, List, Mut -, und der junge Mann, der sich darin hervortat, wurde zum populären Helden"*[11] (Smith, 1943: 93). Aber es war offensichtlich ein gefährliches und riskantes Kriegsspiel, und sogar einige der Besten konnten der Belastung nicht standhalten. Die Kiowa erzählten vom Führer einer Pferderaubgruppe, der nach wenigen Tagen in eine Art Schizophrenie verfiel und von der Wahnvorstellung besessen war, das alle seine Männer Pferde seien. Eines Tages *„hielt er die Gruppe an, stellte die Krieger in einer Reihe auf und untersuchte die Zähne eines jeden Mannes. An einem anderen Tag zwang er alle, im Chor zu wiehern und drohte, jeden Mann niederzuschießen, der nicht wieherte oder ihm nicht gehorchen würde"* (Mishkin, 1940: 33). Diese Episoden könnten amüsant sein, wäre das Ende weniger bestürzend gewesen, denn die Gruppe geriet in einen Hinterhalt, und viele verloren ihr Leben.

Gelegentlich war die Beschaffung von Pferden etwas weniger konventionell. So erzählten die Kiowa von einem alten und angesehenen Mann unter ihnen, der eine unersättliche Begehrlichkeit nach mehr und mehr Pferden entwickelte und zum Kleptomanen wurde, indem er nachts hinausging und die Pferde seiner Nachbarn einsammelte. Am nächsten Tag kamen ihre legitimen Besitzer einfach vorbei und führten sie still wieder zurück - anscheinend wurde der alte Mann *„von seinen amüsierten Stammesbrüdern toleriert"* (ibid: 52).

Der Pferderäuber konnte allein aufbrechen, aber häufiger bestand die Gruppe aus einem Dutzend oder mehr Krieger, und das Unternehmen konnte Tage oder Monate oder manchmal ein Jahr dauern. Jede Jahreszeit war geeignet. Besonders im Winter war ein Capote mit Kapuze oder ein Deckenmantel, im allgemeinen aus einer weißen Decke hergestellt, weil er dann im Schnee nicht auffiel, die bevorzugte Oberbekleidung für solch eine Reise. Pferderaubgruppen verließen ihr Dorf generell zu Fuß und unter dem Schutz der Nacht. Der Anführer oder „Partisan" trug eine Pfeife als Symbol für sein Amt. Die echte Kriegspfeife bestand aus einem geraden Kopf aus Catlinit oder schwarzem Steatit in einheitlicher Linie mit dem hölzernen Stiel (Abb. 35). Es wird behauptet, daß das Feuer in einer solchen, zum Boden zeigenden Pfeife, von wachsamen Feinden schlechter zu erkennen war (Smith, 1943: 95-6). Derartige Pfeifen wurden

---

[11] Der Begriff „Erbeuten" anstatt „Stehlen" wurde von den Blackfeet bevorzugt (Ewers, 1955). James Dempsey wies mich nach meinem Cody-Vortrag ebenfalls auf diesen Punkt hin.

Capturing horses

As DeCost Smith has said, running off the enemies' horses was both legitimate and honorable (Fig. 34): *„As a measure of aggression or reprisal it was doubly effective; it enriched the plunderer while it deprived the plundered of property indispensable to his safety and well-being. A robust, manly pastime, it was also splendid training in the Spartan virtues - patience, cunning, courage - and the young man who excelled in it became a popular hero"*[11] (Smith, 1943: 93). But it was obviously a dangerous and hazardous war-game, and even some of the best cracked under the strain. The Kiowa told of a horse raid leader who after a few days lapsed into some type of schizophrenic condition, obsessed with the delusion that all his men were horses. One day *„he stopped the party, lined up the warriors and examined the teeth of each man. Another day he forced all of them to bray in chorus threatening to shoot any man who did not bray or obey him"* (Mishkin, 1940: 33). These episodes would have been amusing had the outcome been less dismaying, for the party was ambushed and many lost their lives.

Acquisition of horses was, on occasion, somewhat less conventional. Thus, the Kiowa also told of an aged and respected one of their number who developed an insatiable desire to acquire more and more horses developing into kleptomania, such that at nights he would go out and collect his neighbors' horses. The next day their rightful owners would simply come along and quietly lead them away again - apparently the old man *„was tolerated by his amused tribesmen"*! (ibid: 52).

The horse raider might start out alone, but more often the party would consist of a dozen or more, and the enterprise might take days or months or sometimes a year. Any season could be selected and, in winter especially, a hooded capote or blanket coat generally made of a white blanket, was the outer garment favored for such a journey, since it was inconspicuous in the snow. Horse capturing parties generally left home on foot under cover of night, the leader or partisan carrying a pipe as a symbol of his office; the true war pipe, was a straight cylinder of catlinite or black steatite in direct line with the wooden stem (Fig. 35), it being contended that the fire in such a pipe, being pointed toward the ground, was less apt to be seen by lurking enemies (Smith, 1943: 95-6); such pipes were not infrequently consecrated, and at the first stop it was ceremonially smoked.

At night, when the proximity of war parties was suspected, a man would picket one or two of his choicest animals - those trained to war or buffalo running, and racers - close to the front of his lodge. Here they were not only available for instant use, but as the lodges invariably faced east, and the bed of the owner was to the right on entering, horses thus picketed stood so near their owner as he slept that any unusual movement on their part would be

---

[11] The term „capturing" rather than „stealing" was preferred by the Blackfeet (Ewers, 1955). James Dempsey also made this point to me after the Cody Lecture.

nicht selten vom Medizinmann gesegnet, und bei der ersten Rast wurden sie zeremoniell geraucht.

Des Nachts, wenn die Annäherung von Kriegsgruppen vermutet wurde, pfählte ein Mann eines oder zwei seiner erlesensten Tiere - die für den Krieg oder die Bisonjagd und Pferderennen ausgebildet waren - unmittelbar vor seinem Zelt an. Hier waren sie nicht nur für den sofortigen Einsatz verfügbar, sondern da die Zelte ausnahmslos nach Osten ausgerichtet waren und das Bett des Eigentümers sich rechts vom Eingang befand, standen die derart angepflockten Pferde so dicht bei ihrem schlafenden Besitzer, daß jede ungewöhnliche Bewegung auf ihrer Seite ihn wahrscheinlich aufgeweckt hätte. Obwohl es ein riskantes Unternehmen war, sie aus dieser Position zu stehlen, war es dennoch ein Teil des Kriegsspiels. Dabei war das Zerschneiden des Seils eher als das Losbinden die Standard-Methode, so daß kein Zweifel blieb, daß das Tier sich nicht selbst befreit hatte - das baumelnde Seilende war ein Symbol der Verhöhnung des Feindes (Smith, 1943: 104).

Weil der Raub eines festgebundenen Pferdes aus einem feindlichen Lager eine Tat von besonderer Bedeutung war, war mit dem Unternehmen ein bestimmter Symbolismus verbunden, und es wurde als vollständiges Bild oder stilisiert als einfaches Symbol gezeigt. Bei den Blackfeet, wie in Abb. 36 zu sehen, schneidet der Abenteurer Pferde, die nahe bei den Tipis angepflockt sind, los, dann wiederum wird das Losschneiden von einem Messer und einer Hand dargestellt (Abb. 37), dann sind nur die Pflöcke zusammen mit dem durchtrennten Seil zu sehen; sie stehen für die Pferde, die auf diese Weise weggenommen wurden (Abb. 38), und schließlich sieht man nur eine Reihe von gekreuzten Linien (Abb. 39). Diese letztere Darstellung ist tatsächlich die schlichteste von allen, und sie wechselte, Wissler zufolge, zwischen dem Pflock und dem Kreuz, abhängig vom jeweiligen Maler (Wissler, 1911: 41).

An die Erbeutung von Pferden erinnerten oft gefärbte Pferdehaarfransen an der Kleidung eines erfolgreichen Kriegers. Bei der Beschreibung der Tracht des Crow-Häuptlings Deaf Bull (Abb. 40) berichtete DeCost Smith, das an seinem Überwurf *„pinkgefärbte Pferdehaarsträhnen"* befestigt waren, die zwischen Skalplocken angebracht waren und *„wahrscheinlich für im Krieg erbeutete Pferde standen"* (Smith, 1943: 140). Auch als der französische Entdecker Graf d'Otrante 1842 das als Abb. 41 gezeigte Hemd sammelte, erklärte sein Besitzer, ein Blackfeet, daß die daran befestigten Pferdehaarsträhnen vom Feind erbeutete Pferde darstellten.

Es konnten mehrere Hemden lokalisiert werden, die zweifellos eine Fülle von Pferdessymbolen aufweisen - möglicherweise Reitpeitschen, Hufabdrücke und vorwiegend Pferdehaar (Abb. 42). Das läßt vermuten, daß es vielleicht Insignien gab, die einen besonders erfolgreichen Pferderäuber kennzeichneten - obwohl dies anscheinend nie dokumentiert wurde. Ferner glaube ich, daß Haarsträhnen eine Art von Treueschwur darstellten, so wie es bei dem sogenannten Red Cloud Hemd (Abb. 43) der Fall war, wo etwa 68 Pferdehaar-

likely to awaken him. Although to steal them from such a position was a risky business, nevertheless this was all part of the war-game. Cutting, rather than untying the rope was the standard method, and it left no doubt that the animal had not freed itself - the dangling end being a symbol of taunt to the enemy (Smith, 1943: 104).

Because the capture of a tied up horse in an enemy's camp was a deed of special importance, the action had definite symbolism associated with it and it was shown in the full pictured form or conventionalized to a bare symbol. For the Blackfeet, one can see in Fig. 36, the adventurer cutting loose horses picketed near the tipis, then again the cutting represented by a knife and a hand (Fig. 37), then the pickets alone complete with the severed rope as representing the horses so taken (Fig. 38) and finally, just a series of crossed lines (Fig. 39). This last, of course, is really the simplest of all and it alternated, according to Wissler, between the picket stake and cross depending on the individual (Wissler, 1911: 41).

The capture of horses was often commemorated by colored horsehair fringing on the successful warrior's costume. For example, DeCost Smith, in describing the costume of Deaf Bull, a Crow chief (Fig. 40), reported that his tunic had attached „*locks of horsehair dyed pink*", which were interspersed among the scalp lock fringes and „*probably stood for horses captured in war*" (Smith, 1943: 140). Further, when the French explorer, Count d'Otrante collected this shirt in 1842 (Fig. 41), its Blackfeet owner said that the horsehair locks which were attached to it, represented the horses captured from the enemy.

Several shirts have been located which are absolutely replete in horse symbolism - perhaps quirts, horse prints, and a predominance of horsehair (Fig. 42); it suggests that here may have been regalia which designated a particularly successful horse raider - although this appears to have gone unrecorded. I think too that hair-locks might have been used as something of a pledge allegiance - such as on the so-called Red Cloud shirt (Fig. 43) - where some sixty-eight horsehair locks are interspersed between the two hundred and thirty-eight human hair locks.[12]

It was not, however, just the capture of horses which increased a man's standing, thus the gift of horses was one of the best ways of guaranteeing a man's rise to a position of prominence, particularly if he gave them to needy band members (Ewers, 1955: 256). Such generosity was symbolically recorded by the Hidatsa chief, Yellow Bear, who, quite by chance in November 1833, was seen painting a special gift robe by Prince Maximilian. This robe (Fig. 44), Maximilian recorded, was „*decorated with symbols of treasures given away*" (Maximilian, 1839-41, Vol. II: 268), which not only included trade blankets or cloth

---

[12a] Research, Cody. August 1986 and verified with Bill Mercer, Museum intern.
[12b] The Hidatsa Wolf Chief explained the use of colored horsehair as an honor mark among his tribe: "*For the fifth time a war leader (or any member of his party) captured horses (on separate parties) he hung white or colored horse hair on his neck flap... a sixth capture was marked by tying white or colored horse hair on the robe...*" (Gilman and Schneider, 1987: 105).

Strähnen zwischen 238 Menschenhaarlocken eingearbeitet sind.[12]

Nicht nur das Erbeuten von Pferden, verbesserte die Stellung eines Mannes, sondern das Verschenken von Pferden war eine der besten Möglichkeiten, einem Mann den Aufstieg zu einer hervorragenden Position zu sichern, besonders wenn er sie an bedürftige Mitglieder der Gruppe weitergab (Ewers, 1955: 256). Derartige Großzügigkeit wurde symbolisch von dem Hidatsa-Häuptling Yellow Bear dokumentiert, den Prinz Maximilian im November 1833 zufällig beim Bemalen einer speziellen Geschenkrobe beobachtete. Diese Robe (Abb. 44) wurde, wie Maximilian berichtete, *„mit Symbolen von verschenkten Wertgegenständen dekoriert"* (Maximilian, 1839-41, Vol. II: 268), zu denen nicht nur Handelsdecken oder Stoff und Schilde gehörten, sondern auch Reitpeitschen, die stets zusammen mit dem Tier verschenkt wurden. Diese Robe vermittelt uns außerdem einige gute Einblicke in die numerologischen Vorstellungen der Plainsindianer, eine „Hand-eins" oder „Fünf-eins" steht für 6, denn die Gruppierung von Stoff und Peitschen wird sechserweise oder multipliziert mit dieser Zahl vorgenommen.

Ich meine ferner, daß die Reitpeitschen, die auf mehreren Kriegshemden in den Sammlungen zu sehen sind, wahrscheinlich auf Pferde hinweisen, die der Träger des Kleidungsstückes verschenkt hat. All dies legt nahe, daß Freigebigkeit bei den Plainsindianern fast den gleichen Stellenwert wie das mehr kriegerische Coupzählen hatte.

All dies war nicht exklusiv auf männliche Trachten beschränkt. Abb. 45 zeigt ein Foto einer Oglala-Medizinfrau. Dem Fotografen zufolge erzählte sie, daß sie Jahre zuvor einen jüngeren Bruder hatte, der dreimal die Crow überfiel, um Pferde für seine Schwester zu erbeuten. Zusammengenommen schenkte er ihr 10 Pferde, aber beim vierten Überfall fingen die Crow ihn und töteten ihn. Die in Perlen gearbeiteten Hufabdrücke auf ihrem Kleid aus auffälligem rotem Tradecloth stellten eine Erinnerung an die Pferde dar, die er ihr schenkte, während, wie sie erklärte, die beiden Hände, die auf dem Oberteil ihres Kleides zu sehen sind, an seinen letzten Kampf erinnerten (Haberland, 1986: 84-87).

[12a] Untersucht in Cody, August 1986 und verifiziert mit Bill Mercer, Museum intern.
[12b] Der Hidatsa Wolf Chief erklärte, die Verwendung von gefärbtem Pferdehaar sei ein Ehrenzeichen bei seinem Stamm: "*Erbeutete ein Kriegsführer (oder irgendein Mitglied seiner Gruppe) zum fünften Mal Pferde (bei verschiedenen Gelegenheiten), hängte er weißes oder gefärbtes Pferdehaar an seinen Nacken-Flap... Ein sechster Beutezug wurde gekennzeichnet, indem weißes oder gefärbtes Pferdehaar an der Robe befestigt wurde...*" (Gilman and Schneider, 1987: 105).

and shields but quirts which were always given away with the animal. The robe also gives us some good insights into the numerological aspect of Plains Indians, a „hand-one" or „five-one" for six because the grouping of both cloth and quirts is in sixes or multiples of that number.

I think too that the quirts which appear on several warshirts in the collections, probably make reference to the gift of horses by the wearer of the garment. All this suggests that gift-giving among the Plains Indians ranked close to that of the more war-like coup counting.

Neither was all this exclusive to men's costume. Fig. 45 shows a photograph of an Oglala medicine woman. According to the photographer, this lady said that years previously she had a younger brother who three times raided the Crow to capture horses for his sister. Altogether, he made her a gift of ten horses but on the fourth foray, the Crow captured and killed him. The horse tracks worked in beads on her striking red trade cloth dress were a reminder of the horses he had given her while the two hands rendered on the top of her dress, she explained, were to commemorate his last battle (Haberland, 1986: 84-87).

Die Kräfte des Donner

Wie ich bereits erwähnte, wurden Pferde in vielen Piktographien dargestellt, wobei die Konzentration auf das Detail sehr auffällig ist. Zum Beispiel ist im Wintercount von Blue Thunder und anderen Zählungen für 1800-01 die Erbeutung des ersten Hengstes mit Kraushaar aufgezeichnet. Vestal zufolge waren diese Pferde im allgemeinen von dunkler Farbe, so daß ihr Haar versengt wirkte - demzufolge ist der Lakota-Name für sie *„Sung-gu-gu-la"*, was bedeutet *„Pferde mit verbranntem Haar"* (Howard, 1979: 22, und Vestal, 1934: 174).

Einige Pferde wurden in den unwahrscheinlichsten Farben dargestellt (Abb. 46). Sowohl Blackfeet- als auch Cheyenne-Informanten erwähnen jedoch *„blaue Pferde"* - die Sonne ließ sie so wirken, wenn sie schweißbedeckt waren, was natürlich unter den Bedingungen einer Schlacht der Fall war.[13]

Interessanterweise berichtete Dr. J. R. Walker, daß ein blau gezeichnetes Pferd von den Lakota als besonderes Kriegspferd angesehen wurde (Walker, DeMallie und Jahner eds., 1980: 232), und Clark Wissler ging noch einen Schritt weiter, als er in seiner klassischen Arbeit *„Some Protective Designs of the Dakota"* sagte, daß die blaue Farbe des Pferdes auf Verbindungen mit den Kräften des Donners oder den Kräften des Himmels hinwies (Wissler, 1907: 23). Die Verbindung zum Blitz wird durch die Little Big Man-Skizzen - die wahrscheinlich Crazy Horse zeigen - betont. Das Pferd war mit Zickzackmustern bemalt, die die Beine hinunterreichen (Abb. 47); wie früher erwähnt symbolisiert die Tatsache, daß sie an den Enden gegabelt sind, daß der Besitzer durch einen Traum oder eine Vision über eine direkte Verbindung mit den Kräften des Donners verfügte (Taylor, McCaskill ed., 1989: 239).

Der Symbolismus ist jedoch weitaus umfangreicher und scheint erheblich über bildliche Darstellungen hinauszugehen. Der Lakota-Historiker Amos Bad Heart Bull gab einige eindeutige Hinweise auf die Kräfte des Donners und die Kriegsführung. Abb. 48 (Blish, 1967: 204) zeigt zwei Reiter, die ihre Kräfte durch ein ungewöhnliches Erlebnis von den Donnergöttern erhalten hatten (Blish, 1967: 204). Alle Zeichnungen auf Gesicht und Körper und auf den Leibern der Pferde stellen Kräfte des Sturms dar. Besonders interessant ist, daß das Haar der Männer - wie die auffällige Anordnung an der Stirn verrät - mit Hilfe einer klebrigen Pflanze frisiert war, die in enger Verbindung mit der Kraft des Donners stand. Es wurde gesagt, daß der Blitz das Haar auf diese Weise zurichtete, wenn er einen Menschen traf. Die Pferde wurden auf dieselbe Weise geschmückt, Stirnlocke und Schweif waren mit Hülsenfruchtschalen bedeckt. Bei dieser Pflanze handelt es sich höchstwahrscheinlich um *Silphium laciniatum*, allgemein Kompaß-Pflanze genannt. Die Lakota nannten sie *chanshishilya*, was bedeutet, *„eine Pflanze aus der Gummi hervorquillt"*. Die Omaha berichteten, daß dort, wo diese Pflanze reichlich vorhanden war, bevorzugt Blitze einschlugen.

---

[13] Erörterungen mit Father Peter Powell und John C. Ewers, Smithsonian Institution, Washington, D. C., July 1989.

Thunder Powers

Of course, as I have already mentioned, horses were rendered in many pictographic images, and the eye for detail is very apparent. For example, in the Blue Thunder and other Winter Counts, for 1800-01, the capture of the first curly-hair stallion is depicted. According to Vestal, these horses were generally dark in color whose hair appeared to be singed - hence the Lakota name for them, *Sung-gu-gu-la*, meaning „*horses with burnt hair*" (Howard, 1979: 22, and Vestal, 1934: 174).

Some horses were rendered in the most unlikely colors (Fig. 46). Both Blackfeet and Cheyenne informants, however, did refer to „blue horses" - it was the way the sun caught them when sweating, which, of course, would be the situation in battle conditions.[13] Interestingly, according to Dr. J. R. Walker, a horse depicted in blue was considered by the Lakota to be a special warhorse (Walker, DeMallie and Jahner eds. 1980: 232), and Clark Wissler took this one stage further when, in his classic „*Some Protective Designs of the Dakota*", he said that the blue color of the horse indicated connections with thunder powers or the powers of the sky (Wissler, 1907: 23). The lightning connection is emphasized by the sketches of Little Big Man - probably of Crazy Horse - showing the horse painted with zigzag designs down the legs (Fig. 47); as mentioned earlier, the fact that they are forked at the ends, symbolizes that the owner had direct communication through a dream or vision with the thunder powers (Taylor, McCaskill ed., 1989: 239).

The symbolism is, however, far more complex than this and seems to extend well beyond the painted images. The Lakota historian, Amos Bad Heart Bull, made some definite references to these thunder powers and the warpath. In Fig. 48 (Blish, 1967: 204), are shown two riders who, through an unusual experience, have received their powers from the thunder gods. All the markings of face and body and of the body of the horse represent storm forces. Of particular interest is that the men's hair - giving the peculiar arrangement at the front - was so arranged by use of a gum-like plant which was closely associated with thunder power, for it was said that this is the way lightning arranges the hair when it strikes a person. This style of decoration was extended to the horses, both its forelock and the tail being covered with a leguminous plant material. This plant is almost certainly *Silphium laciniatum*, commonly referred to as Compass plant. The Lakota called it *chanshishilya*, which means „*a plant from which gum oozes*". It was reported by the Omaha that where this plant abounds, lightning was very prevalent and the dried plant was burned by them during electric storms so that its smoke might act as a charm to avert lightning strikes (Gilmore, 1919: 132). Note that the chest and rump of the horses not only have hail painting but also a forked lightning symbol down the legs,

---

[13] Discussions with Father Peter Powell and John C. Ewers, Smithsonian Institution, Washington, D. C., July 1989.

In Gewittern verbrannten sie die trockene Pflanze, denn ihr Rauch diente möglicherweise als Zauber gegen Blitzeinschläge (Gilmore, 1919: 132). Man beachte, daß Brust und Rumpf der Pferde nicht nur Hagelbemalung aufweisen, sondern auch ein gegabeltes Blitzsymbol die Beine hinunterverläuft, und die Reiter zeigen dasselbe Motiv auf ihren Gesichtern. Über den weitergehenden Symbolismus der verknoteten Schweife wird nichts berichtet; die üblichen Adlerfedern[14] wurden durch dünne Stäbe oder Zweige ersetzt, deren Enden nach oben zeigen.

Während Blish über deren Symbolismus nichts berichtet, erzählte mir vor einigen Jahren Professor Edwin Kessler von der University of Oklahoma, ein Experte für Blitze, von einem aufregenden Erlebnis, daß er während eines Gewitters gehabt hatte. Ich denke es könnte helfen, diese Zeichnungen von Mann und Pferd von Amos Bad Heart Bull zu erklären. Kessler befand sich während eines Gewitters am Rand eines aktiven Vulkans in Costa Rica, und das starke elektrische Kraftfeld ließ ihm die Haare zu Berge stehen; könnte dies der Zustand sein, der von den stehenden Zweigen repräsentiert wird?

Abb. 49 zeigt eine andere Skizze von Bad Heart Bull (Blish, 1967: 208, 482, 485). Pferd und Mann sind mit Hagel- und gegabelten Blitzsymbolen bemalt. Die gegabelten Enden eines Blitzsymbols sind, man erinnere sich, ein Hinweis darauf, daß der Mann in direkter Verbindung mit den Kräften des Donners gestanden hat; und hier sehen wir nicht nur die aufrechten Stäbe im Schweif wie im Bild bevor, sondern jetzt hat der Mann sie im Haar, und sie stecken auch in der Stirnlocke des Pferdes. Man stelle sich einen Plainsindianer der alten Zeit während seiner Visionssuche vor, hoch auf einer Hügelkuppe, eine Pfeife in der Hand, und ein nahendes Gewitter... Plötzlich, infolge eines starken elektrischen Kraftfeldes, das sich, wie wir wissen, zwischen hoch aufgeladenen Wolken und der Erdoberfläche aufbaut, standen dem Krieger die Haare zu Berge. Er wird <u>nicht</u> vom Blitz getroffen - er überlebt! Konnte sich ein solcher Mann nicht auf eine außergewöhnliche Beziehung zu den Kräften des Donners berufen - die auch auf sein Pferd übertragen wurde?[15]

---

[14] Jaw pflegte sein erfolgreiches Pferd mit Federn in Schweif oder Mähne oder einem Band aus rotem Stoff zu belohnen (Densmore, 1918: 388).

[15] Die Kräfte von Donner und Blitz werden von den Lakota noch immer gefürchtet. In Porcupine auf der Pine Ridge Reservation erzählte Calvin Jumping Bull dem Autor im Juli 1988, daß der Sendemast der Radiostation auf der Reservation mit einer Adlerfeder (die vom Medizinmann gesegnet worden war) geschmückt wurde, um die häufigen Blitzeinschläge abzuwehren - offenbar war diese Maßnahme wirksam! (Es gibt wahrscheinlich einige gute wissenschaftliche Gründe dafür.) Calvin Jumping Bull berichtete mir auch, daß die Sioux einen scherzhaften Spruch über Blitze haben: *„Mahpiya wicaktepi kin ecela otokicun sice."*, was übersetzt heißt: „Wenn du von einem Blitz getroffen wirst, kannst du nicht zurückschlagen."

and the riders have the same motif on their faces. Not reported, is the further symbolism associated with the tied tails; instead of the usual eagle feathers,[14] these have been replaced by fine sticks or twigs, the ends tending upwards.

While the symbolism was not reported by Blish, some years ago Professor Edwin Kessler of the University of Oklahoma and an expert on lightning, told me of one disconcerting experience which he had had relating to a thunderstorm, which I think could help explain these drawings of man and horse by Amos Bad Heart Bull. Kessler was at the edge of an active volcano in Costa Rica during a thunderstorm and the strong electric field caused his hair to stand on end; could this be a condition represented by the standing twigs?

Fig. 49 shows another sketch by Bad Heart Bull (Blish, 1967: 208, 482, 485). The horse and man are painted with hail and forked lightning symbols; the forked ends of a lightning symbol, remember, indicates that the man has had direct rapport with the thunder-powers and here, not only do we have the upright sticks in the tail as before, but now the man has them in his hair and they are also in the forelock of the horse's head. One should imagine an old-time Plains Indian on his vision quest, high on a hilltop and pipe in hand, a thunderstorm in the vicinity... Suddenly, due to the intense electric field which we know builds up between the high potential cloud and the surface of the earth, the warrior's hair stands on end. There is no lightning strike - he survives! Surely, such a person could lay claim to unusual rapport with the thunder-powers - which he transferred also to his horse?[15]

---

[14] Jaw's custom was to reward his successful horse with feathers in the tail or mane or a band of red list-cloth (Densmore, 1918: 388).

[15] Thunder and lightning power is still held in awe by the Lakota. While at Porcupine on the Pine Ridge Reservation in July 1988, Calvin Jumping Bull told the author that a radio mast transmitter on the Reservation had been embellished with an eagle feather (blessed by the medicine man) to stop the frequent lightning strikes - apparently it was effective! (There are some probable good scientific reasons for this). Calvin Jumping Bull also told me that the Sioux have a jesting statement about lightning: „Mahpiya wicaktepi kin ecela otokicun sice" which translates to „If you are struck by the lightning there is no way of getting even"!

47) Sketch by Little Big Man of Crazy Horse (?) in battle. Note the zigzag lines painted on the legs of the horse, as representative of thunder powers (For illustration, see Johnson, 1891: 115).

47) Skizze von Little Big Man, die Crazy Horse (?) in der Schlacht zeigt. Man beachte die Zickzacklinien, die als Repräsentation der Kräfte des Donners auf die Beine des Pferdes gemalt sind. (Wegen der Illustration siehe Johnson, 1891: 115.)

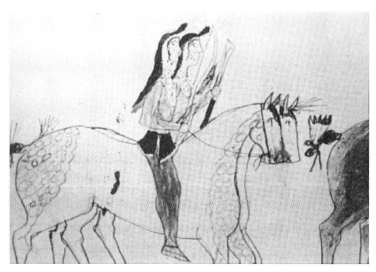

48) Two riders who have received their powers from *Wakinyan*, the Thunder God. Note that all the markings refer to storm forces while the men's hair has been arranged by use of a gum-like substance which itself has lightning connections (see text). (Blish, 1967: 204).

48) Zwei Reiter, die ihre Kräfte von *Wakinyan*, dem Donnergott, empfangen haben. Man beachte, da· alle Markierungen auf die Kräfte des Sturms hinweisen, während das Haar der Männer mittels einer gummiartigen Substanz frisiert wurde, die selbst in Verbindung mit dem Blitz steht. (Siehe Text.) Blish, 1967:204.)

49) Lightning symbols on horse and man. The lightning is forked at the ends, symbolic of the fact that the wearer has had direct rapport with the thunder powers. Note the upright sticks in the man's hair and on the head and tail of the horse. (See Blish, 1967: 208). Compare with Fig. 48. (Note both this and Fig. 48 are by Amos Bad Heart Bull).

49) Blitzsymbole auf Pferd und Reiter. Der Blitz ist an den Enden gegabelt, Symbol für die Tatsache, daß der Träger direkte Verbindung mit den Kräften des Donners hatte. Man beachte die aufrechten Stäbe im Haar des Mannes und auf dem Kopf und im Schweif des Pferdes. (Siehe Blish, 1967: 208) Vergleiche dies mit Abb. 48. (Diese und Abb. 48 stammen von Amos Bad Heart Bull.)

50) The taking of scalps and capture of weapons is symbolically represented on this Blackfeet horse. Sketch by the Piegan Red Plume (See Wissler, 1913: 457).

50) Das Nehmen von Skalps und die Erbeutung von Waffen wird symbolisch auf diesem Blackfeet-Pferd dargestellt. Skizze des Piegan Red Plume. (Siehe Wissler, 1913: 457.)

51) Billy Jones (Gros Ventre) singing at the Grass Dance, Fort Belknap, July 1905. The pictographic representation of weapons on the flank of his horse signify his various war exploits. (Photograph, courtesy of R. A. Pohrt, Michigan).

51) Billy Jones (Gros Ventre) singt während des Gras-Tanzes in Fort Belknap, Juli 1905. Die piktographischen Darstellungen von Waffen auf den Flanken seines Pferdes demonstrieren seine verschiedenen Kriegstaten. (Foto mit Genehmigung von R. A. Pohrt, Michigán.)

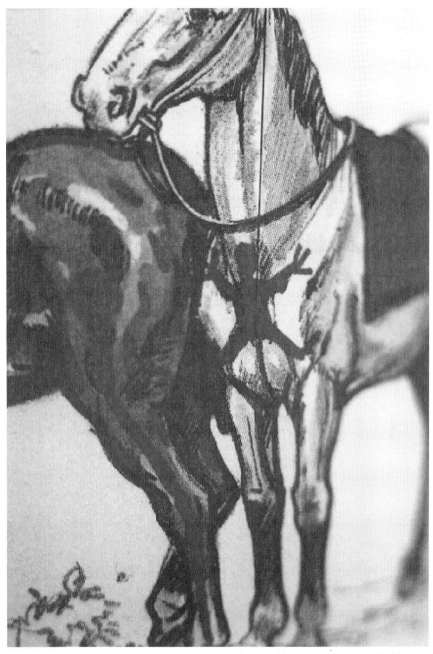

52) Riding down a man in battle is a feat symbolically stated by this pictograph. Blackfeet, and after a sketch by Red Plume (Wissler, 1913: 457).

52) Das Niederreiten eines Mannes in der Schlacht ist eine bravouröse Tat, die diese Piktographie symbolisch bezeugt. Blackfeet. Nach einer Skizze von Red Plume. (Wissler, 1913: 457.)

53) Symbols of the dragon-fly and lizard are painted on this Arapaho horse - hard to hit and difficult to kill creatures (Petersen, 1988: 64).

53) Symbole der Libelle und der Eidechse sind auf dieses Arapaho-Pferd gemalt - schwer zu treffende und zu tötende Kreaturen. (Petersen, 1988: 64.)

54) Dragon-fly symbols were particularly favored by the Cheyenne and Lakota and they are invariably painted in blue. Both creature and color are highly symbolic (See text). This is a Cheyenne horse. (Powell, 1981: opp. 120).

54) Libellensymbole waren besonders bei den Cheyenne und Lakota beliebt, und sie wurden stets in blau gemalt. Tier und Farbe waren höchst symbolisch. (Siehe Text.) Dies ist ein Cheyennepferd. (Powell, 1981: opp. 120.)

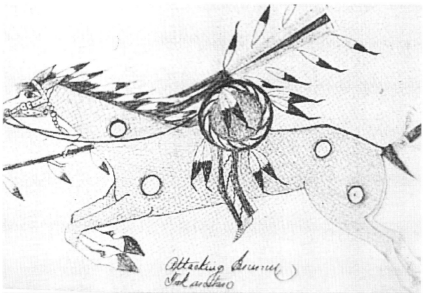

55 and 56) Sacred hoop symbol on elk and horses. This symbol was used to evoke powers of immortality (See Blish, 1967: 199 and Penney, IN Maurer et al, 1992: 77).

55 und 56) Das sakrale Reifensymbol auf Wapitihirsch und Pferden. Dieses Symbol diente der Beschwörung von Kräften der Unsterblichkeit. (Siehe Blish, 1967: 199, sowie Penney, IN Maurer et al, 1992: 77.)

Symbolische Bemalung

Fletcher und La Flesche führten aus, daß Omaha-Männer häufig ihre Pferde bemalten, entweder um eine mutige Tat darzustellen oder um eine Vision zu repräsentieren (Fletcher und LaFlesche, 1911: 352-3).

Dies traf selbstverständlich auf die meisten Plainsstämme zu, obwohl die Schwerpunkte etwas variierten. Abb. 50 zeigt beispielsweise eine Skizze von Red Plume, einem von Wisslers Blackfeet-Informanten. Zu sehen sind Waffen und ein Skalp, auf Flanke und Seite eines Pferdes gemalt. Die Erbeutung der Waffe eines Feindes, insbesondere eines Gewehrs, wie hier gezeigt, wurde bei den Blackfeet als höchste Kriegsehre angesehen, während das Nehmen eines Skalps im allgemeinen an zweiter Stelle stand. Die Gros Ventre - ein Stamm, der eng mit den Blackfeet verwandt ist - hatten anscheinend einen ähnlichen Brauch (Abb. 51). An andere Taten, wie etwa das Niederreiten eines Mannes im Kampf, erinnerten die Blackfeet durch das Bild eines Mannes mit gespreizten Beinen, gemalt auf die Brust oder den vorderen Teil des Pferdes (Abb. 52) - eine Sitte, die auch von den Hidatsa berichtet wird (Wilson, 1916: 38).

Während die Sioux, Cheyenne und Arapaho zweifellos denselben Symbolismus hatten, legten sie anscheinend tatsächlich besonderen Wert auf gemalte Symbole, die dem Tier Kraft im Kampf gaben, so sollte eine Darstellung von Hörnern der Pronghorn-Antilope ihm die Schnelligkeit und Überlebenskraft von einem der typischsten Tiere der Plains verleihen. Abb. 53 zeigt ein von einem Arapaho gemaltes Pferd. Die Symbole wurden von Karen Petersen interpretiert. Sie stellen eine Libelle dar, damit das Tier schwer zu treffen war, und eine Eidechse, um ihm Beweglichkeit und Schnelligkeit zu verleihen (Petersen, 1988: 64). Libellensymbole wurden besonders von den Cheyenne bevorzugt (Abb. 54) - sie wurden aber auch von den Lakota benutzt, die mit vielen symbolischen Konzepten übereinstimmten - sie waren Zeichen für die Kräfte des Überlebens. So hatten die Cheyenne beobachtet, daß die Libelle aus einer Wasserlarve schlüpfte, und da, wie Moore feststellte, tiefes Wasser mit dem Nachthimmel und dem Tod assoziiert wurde und bekannt war, daß die blaue Libelle diese tiefen, dunklen Kräfte überwinden und aus der Larve entfliehen konnte, war sie das *„Sinnbild für den Schutz gegen den Tod"* (Moore, 1974: 158).

Eine Reihe von Bad Heart Bulls Bildern (Blish, 1967: 442) zeigen Pferde mit einer reifenähnlichen Darstellung auf Seiten oder Flanken. (Abb. 55) Wie Nachforschungen zeigen, war der Kreis oder Reifen, mit oder ohne Mittelpunkt, ein sehr wichtiges religiöses Motiv für die Lakota, und wenn er in einem bestimmten Kontext benutzt wurde, etwa auf Kleidungsstücken des Geistertanzes - wurde er als Symbol für Schutz oder Unsterblichkeit angesehen. Demzufolge identifizierten die Lakota den Traum- oder Geisthirsch mit einem solchen Motiv, und Wissler berichtete, daß solche Kreaturen als unsterblich und übernatürlich angesehen wurden. Hier (Abb. 5) scheint diese Vorstellung auf bestimmte Pferde ausgedehnt worden zu sein.

Wie ich zuvor erwähnte, wählten die Blackfeet bestimmte Pferde für den

Symbolic painting

Fletcher and La Flesche make the point that Omaha men frequently painted their horses to represent a valorous deed or in a manner intended as a representation of a vision (Fletcher and La Flesche, 1911: 352-3).

Clearly, this was also true of most Plains tribes, although the emphasis varied somewhat. Fig. 50, for example, shows a sketch by Red Plume, one of Wissler's Blackfeet informants, showing weapons and a scalp painted on the horse's flank and side. Capture of an enemy's arms, particularly a gun as shown here, was considered to be the highest Blackfeet war honor, while taking a scalp was generally regarded as second in rank. The Gros Ventre - a tribe closely related to the Blackfeet - also used a similar custom it seems (Fig. 51). Other Blackfeet exploits, such as riding down a man in battle, were commemorated by the figure of a man with legs splayed out painted on the chest or front part of the horse (Fig. 52) - a custom also reported for the Hidatsa (Wilson, 1916: 38).

While the Sioux, Cheyenne and Arapaho undoubtedly used the same symbolism, they do seem to have put emphasis on painted symbols to give power to the animal in battle, such as a rendering of horns of the prong-horned antelope to impart the same swiftness and survival powers of one of the purest of Plains animals. Fig. 53 shows a horse painted by an Arapaho, the symbols interpreted by Karen Petersen as a dragon-fly to make the animal hard to hit and a lizard to provide activeness and swift motion (Petersen, 1988: 64). Dragon-fly symbols were particularly favored by the Cheyenne (Fig. 54) (but were also used by the Lakota who shared many symbolic concepts) - they were symbolic of powers of survival. Thus, the Cheyenne observed that the dragon-fly hatched from an aquatic nymph and as Moore has observed, because deep water was associated with the night sky and death, the blue dragon-fly which was known to overcome these deep, dark water forces and escape on hatching was „emblematic of protection against death" (Moore, 1974: 158).

A number of Bad Heart Bull's paintings (Blish, 1967: 442) show horses with a hoop-like figure rendered on their sides or flanks (Fig. 55). Research suggests that the circle or hoop, with or without a central spot, was a very important religious motif to the Lakota, and when used in a certain context, such as on Ghost-dance garments, was considered a symbol of protection or immortality. In consequence, the Lakota identified the dream or spirit elk with such a motif, Wissler reporting that such creatures were considered immortal and supernatural. (Fig. 56), the idea seems to be extended to certain horses.

As I mentioned earlier, the Blackfeet designated certain horses for the transporting of important Medicine Bundles. Wissler reports that the Thunder Pipe Bundle was transported by a horse which had a stripe of red painted across its forehead and down its nose, the mane and tail were painted red, a zigzag line ending in a fork runs down the hind and fore quarter, while red dots on the neck and collar and on the hind quarter, complete the painting (Wissler, 1912 (a): 146). The zigzag ending in a horseshoe, is called the Eagle

Transport der bedeutenden Medizinbündel aus. Wissler berichtet, daß das Donnerpfeifenbündel von einem Pferd transportiert wurde, das mit einem Streifen roter Farbe quer über die Stirn und hinunter zu seiner Nase bemalt worden war. Mähne und Schweif waren rot gefärbt. Eine am Ende gegabelte Zickzacklinie verläuft hinten und vorn hinunter, während rote Punkte auf Hals und Nacken und auf dem Hinterteil die Bemalung vervollständigen (Wissler, 1912 (a): 146). Die an einem Huf endende Zickzacklinie wurde Adlerklaue genannt und ähnelte jener auf der Robe des Medizinpfeifenbesitzers; sie weist auf die Kommunikation mit den Kräften des Donners hin.

Es mangelt an Unterlagen über andere wichtige Bündel. Eine prächtige Ausrüstung im Museum of Mankind, London, jedoch, die anscheinend Teil der Insignien des Eigentümers des sehr alten und höchst symbolischen Biberbündels ist, ist mit einem Pferdemotiv versehen, das detaillierte und höchst bedeutsame Bemalungen trägt (Taylor, 1993: 77). Hier beziehen sich vier der Motive, mit denen das Pferd bemalt ist, höchstwahrscheinlich auf die vier Phasen des Mondes. Anscheinend zeigen sie ihn als Vollmond, zunehmend, abnehmend und als Sichel. Interessant ist, daß einige Blackfeetinformanten Clark Wissler erzählten, daß das Bündel einst bei jedem Vollmond geöffnet wurde. Dies geschah ferner während des Winters - wenn die Bisons selten waren. Es wurde berichtet, daß von den Biberbündelbesitzern erwartet wurde, dem Mond besondere Aufmerksamkeit zu widmen, von dem, wie behauptet wurde, Informationen zu erlangen waren, um das Wetter vorherzusagen - eine Hauptaufgabe der Biberbündelbesitzer. Wenn der Mond aussah, als lehne er sich zurück, wurde das Wetter mild, neigte er sich „nach vorn", wurde es kalt, während Kreise von weißen Wolken um den Mond darauf hinwiesen, daß sich ein warmer Chinook näherte. Eine Lieder-Serie, die nur gesungen werden durfte, wenn dem Volk eine Hungersnot drohte, wurde *„Beschwörung-des-Büffels-Lieder"* genannt (Wissler, 1912 (a): 207). Es ist sehr wahrscheinlich, daß die konische Darstellung mit dem runden Oberteil, die auf das Hinterbein des Heiligen Pferdes gemalt ist (Taylor 1993: 77), auf diesen Teil des Rituals hinweist, weil für die Blackfeet berichtet wurde, daß ein Komet ein Zeichen für Hungersnot und Krankheit war - eine Vorstellung, die viele Nationen teilten und die für die Blackfeet besonders bedeutsam war, die 1854, 1879 und 1883-84 wegen des Ausbleibens der Bisons beziehungsweise der fehlenden Rindfleischrationen der Regierung vom Verhungern bedroht waren. Daher denke ich, daß wir ziemlich sicher sein können, daß dies die Bemalung eines Pferdes war, das mit dem Blackfeet-Biberbündel in Verbindung stand.

Claw and was similar to that on the robe of the Medicine Pipe owner suggesting communication with thunder-powers.

Data is lacking on other important bundles. However, a magnificent outfit in the Museum of Mankind, London, which seems part of the regalia of the owner of the ancient and highly symbolic Beaver Bundle, has on it a motif of a horse bearing detailed and highly significant paintings (Taylor, 1993: 77). Here, four of the motifs painted on the horse almost certainly make reference to four phases of the moon, seemingly showing it full, waxing, waning and in crescent. Of interest is that some Blackfeet informants told Clark Wissler, that formerly the Bundle was opened at each full moon. Further, during the winter (at times when buffalo were scarce), it was reported that Beaver Bundle owners were expected to give particular attention to the moon, which it was claimed could give information which helped with weather forecasting - a major responsibility of the Beaver Bundle owner. Thus, if the moon appeared to lean backwards, the weather was going to be mild, „forward" cold, while circles of white cloud around the moon indicated that a warm chinook was forecast. One series of songs which could only be sung when the people were facing starvation was called „charming-the-buffalo songs" (Wissler, 1912 (a): 207). It is quite probable that the cone-like figure with a round top painted on the back leg of the sacred horse (Taylor 1993: 77), is a reference to this part of the ritual since it has been reported for the Blackfeet, that a comet was a sign of famine and illness - a sentiment shared by many nations and particularly meaningful to the Blackfeet who in 1854, 1879 and 1883-4 faced starvation due to the non-appearance of the buffalo or government-issued beef. I think, therefore, that we can be fairly certain that this was one way of painting a horse associated with the Blackfeet Beaver Bundle.

57 and 58) The universal catastrophe of the crash of horses! Fig. 57, Tapisserie de Bayeux showing scene from the Battle of Hastings in 1066 and Fig. 58, death of a Cheyenne horse (Powell, 1981: opp. 538).

57 und 58) Die universelle Katastrophe des Zusammenpralls von Pferden. Abb. 57 zeigt auf der Tapisserie de Bayeux eine Szene aus der Schlacht von Hastings 1066. Abb. 58 zeigt den Tod eines Cheyenne-Pferdes. (Powell, 1981: opp. 538.)

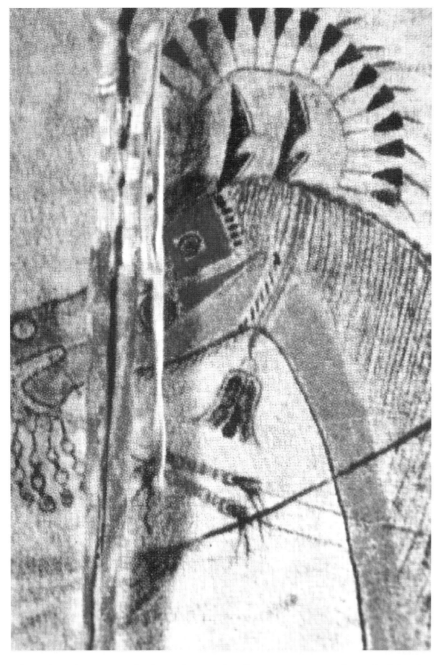

59) Head regalia on a Mandan horse. Painting by Mato-tope, circa 1830, from a buffalo robe (Linden Museum, Stuttgart. Catalogue no. 2).

59) Kopfinsignien eines Mandanpferdes, gemalt von Mato-tope, ca. 1830, auf einer Büffelrobe. (Linden Museum, Stuttgart. Katalog-Nr. 2.)

60) The Crow warrior „He-who-jumps-over-everyone"; painting by George Catlin, 1832. Note the warbonnet on the horse (See Taylor 1994: 201).

60) Der Crow-Krieger „He-who-jumps-over-everyone", gemalt von George Catlin, 1832. Man beachte die Kriegshaube des Pferdes. (Siehe Taylor, 1994: 201.)

61) A Crow horse „mask" and head ornament. The mask is made of buffalo hide, cut black feathers, black and white pony beads, red stroud cloth and bells. This is the way the „bridle" shown in Fig. 33 would be used on the horse (Courtesy, Richard Edwards, Ohio).

61) Eine Crow-Pferde"maske" und -Kopfdekoration. Die Maske ist aus Bisonhaut hergestellt und mit beschnittenen, schwarzen Federn, schwarzen und weißen Pony-Beads, rotem, grobem Wollstoff und Glöckchen versehen. Auf diese Weise wurde das „Zaumzeug", das in Abb. 33 gezeigt wird, am Pferd verwendet. (Genehmigt von Richard Edwards, Ohio.)

62) A double horse „shield" and associated woman's saddle. (Collected by the Rev. Henry Spalding about 1846 and now in the collections in Spalding Park, Idaho). Photograph by Bill Holm.

62) Ein Pferde-Doppel-"Schild" zusammen mit einem Frauen-Sattel. (Gesammelt von Rev. Henry Spalding um 1846 und heute in den Sammlungen in Spalding Park, Idaho). Foto von Bill Holm.

63) Two Sioux riders replete in thunder power symbolism. See Figs. 48 and 49. Sketch by Amos Bad Heart Bull (Blish, 1967).

63) Zwei Sioux-Reiter, erfüllt mit Donnerkraft-Symbolismus. Siehe Abb. 48 und 49. Skizze von Amos Bad Heart Bull. (Blish, 1967.)

Abschließende Bemerkungen

Dies ist nur ein kurzer Überblick über den Symbolismus, der mit dem Pferd in der Plainsindianerkultur in Verbindung stand - ein faszinierendes Thema. All diese symbolischen Konzepte stellen ebenso bestimmte Überlegungen bezüglich solcher Dinge wie Verpflichtungen, Leistungen, Rang, Status und Machtpositionen in der Hierarchie des Stammes dar, wie Parallelen mit anderen Kulturen, bei der Abbildung von Episoden, die mit Pferden zu tun haben, wie etwa dem Zusammenprall von Pferden, beispielsweise in Darstellungen des Mittelalters (Abb. 57 und 58). Es gäbe noch viel mehr zu berücksichtigen: magische Formeln bei der Zucht und damit verbundener Schmuck, Behandlung und Rituale durch die Pferdemedizinmänner, weitere Einzelheiten über Kriegsmedizinen und piktographische Darstellungen von Kriegsehren, inklusive Insignien für den Kopf (Abbildungen 59, 60 und 61). Die Bezahlungen bei der Übertragung von zeremoniellen Insignien, Pferderüstungen, die Schabracke (Abb. 15), der Doppelschild (Abb. 62), Ausschmückungen von Schweif und Mähne, der Symbolismus der Kraft des Donners (Abb. 63) – all dies und viel mehr.

Concluding remarks

This is just a brief survey of symbolism associated with the horse in Plains Indian culture - a fascinating subject. All these symbolic concepts make definite statements with regard to such things as obligations, achievements, rank, status and power positions within the hierarchy of the tribe - as well as parallels with other cultures in depicting horse-related episodes, such as the crash of horses in, for example, medieval paintings (Figs. 57 and 58). There is much more that could be considered - magical breeding formulas and associated embellishments, treatment and rituals by the Horse Medicine Men, more details on war medicines and pictographic representation of war honors including head regalia (Figs. 59, 60 and 61). Values in the transfer of ceremonial regalia, horse armor, the caparison (Fig. 15), double shield (Fig. 62), accoutrements in the tail and mane, thunder-power symbolism (Fig. 63) – all this and much more.

Bibliography and suggested further reading

Blish, Helen H.	1967	„A Pictographic History of the Oglala Sioux". University of Nebraska Press. Lincoln, Nebraska.
Boller, Henry A.	1868	„Among the Indians. Eight Years in the Far West: 1858-1866. Embracing Sketches of Montana and Salt Lake". Philadelphia.
Bradley, James H.	1923	„Characteristics, habits and customs of the Blackfeet Indians". Montana Historical Society. Contrib., Vol. 9
Brasser, Ted J.	1987	„By the Power of their Dreams" IN „The Spirit Sings". McClelland and Stewart. Toronto.
Denig, Edwin Thompson	1930	„Indian Tribes of the Upper Missouri". Edited by J. N. B. Hewitt. Extract from 46th Annual Report of the Bureau of American Ethnology, Smithsonian Institution, Washington, D. C.
Densmore, Frances	1918	„Teton Sioux Music". Bureau of American Ethnology. Bulletin 61. Smithsonian Institution. Washington D. C.
Ewers, John C.	1955	„The Horse in Blackfoot Indian Culture". Bureau of American Ethnology. Bulletin 159. Smithsonian Institution, Washington D. C.
Fletcher, Alice C. and La Flesche, Francis	1911	„The Omaha Tribe". Bureau of American Ethnology. 27th Annual Report. Smithsonian Institution, Washington D. C.
Gilman, Carolyn and Schneider, Mary Jane	1987	„The Way to Independence". Minnesota Historical Society Press, St. Paul.
Gilmore, Melvin R.	1919	„Uses of Plants by the Indians of the Missouri River Region". Bureau of American Ethnology. 33rd Annual Report. Smithsonian Institution, Washington D. C.
Haberland, Wolfgang	1986	„Ich, Dakota: Pine Ridge Reservation 1909". Dietrich Reimer Verlag, Berlin.

Haines, Francis	1938	„Where did the Plains Indians get their horses?". Amer. Anthrop. n. s. Vol. 40. No. 1.
	1938	„The northward spread of horses among the Plains Indians". Amer. Anthrop. n. s. Vol. 40. No. 3.
Hartmann, Horst	1973	„Die Plains- und Prärieindianer Nordamerikas". Museum für Völkerkunde, Berlin.
Henry, Alexander and Thompson, David (Coues ed.)	1897	„New Light on the Early History of the Greater Northwest. The manuscript journals of Alexander Henry and David Thompson 1799-1814". Edited by Elliott Coues. 3 Vols. New York.
Hoig, Stan	1974	„The Western Odyssey of John Simpson Smith: Frontiersman, Trapper, Trader and Interpreter". The Arthur H. Clark Company, Glendale, California.
Howard, James H.	1979	„The British Museum Winter Count". British Museum, Occasional Paper No. (4). Department of Ethnography, London.
Johnson, W. Fletcher	1891	„Life of Sitting Bull and History of the Indian War of 1890-91". Edgewood Publishing Company
Keyser, James D.	1977	„Writing-on-Stone: Rock Art on the Northwestern Plains". Canadian Journal of Archaeology, No. 1.
Keyser, James D.	1987	„A Lexicon for Historic Plains Indian Rock Art: Increasing Interpretive Potential" IN Plains Anthropologist, Vol. 32, number 115.
Kurz, Rudolph	1937	„Journal of Rudolph Friederich Kurz". Edited by J. N. B. Hewitt. Translated by Myrtis Jarrell. Bureau of American Ethnology. Bulletin 115. Smithsonian Institution, Washington, D. C.
Lewis, Meriwether and Clark, William (Coues ed.)	1893	„The History of the Lewis and Clark Expedition". Edited by Elliott Coues. Francis P. Harper. 3 Vols.

Lowie, Robert H. 1909 „The Assiniboine". Anthro. Papers of the American Museum of Natural History. Vol. IV. Pt. 1, New York.

1922 „Crow Indian Art". Anthrop. Papers of the American Museum of Natural History. Vol. XXI. Part IV., New York.

McClintock, Walter 1923 „Old Indian Trails". Constable and Company Limited, London.

1968 „The Old North Trail" (Bison Book Reprint). University of Nebraska Press. Lincoln and London.

Maurer, Evan M. et al 1992 „Visions of the People: A Pictorial History of Plains Indian Life". The Minneapolis Institute of Arts, Minn.

Maximilian, Prince of Wied 1839-41 „Reise in das Innere Nord-America in den Jahren 1832 bis 1834". Coblenz.

Maximilian, Prince of (Thwaites ed.) 1906 „Early Western Travels 1748-1846: Wied Part II of Maximilian, Prince of Wied's Travels in the Interior of North America 1832-1834". Vol. XXIII. Edited by Reuben Gold Thwaites. The Arthur H. Clark Company, Cleveland, Ohio.

Mishkin, Bernard 1940 „Rank and Warfare Among the Plains Indians". University of Washington Press. Seattle and London.

Moore, John Hartwell 1974 „A Study of Religious Symbolism among the Cheyenne Indians". Ph. D. Thesis, New York University.

Penney, David W. and Stouffer, Janet 1986 „Horse Imagery in Native American Arts". The Detroit Institute of Arts, Bulletin 62. No. 1. pp. 18-25.

Petersen, Karen Daniels 1988 „American Pictographic Images. Alexander Gallery and Morning Star Gallery, New York.

Point, Father Nicolas (Donnelly trans.) 1967 „Wilderness Kingdom". Translated by Joseph P. Donnelly, S. J., Michael Joseph, London.

Powell, Father Peter J.	1981	„People of the Sacred Mountain". 2 Vols. Harper & Row, Publishers, Inc., New York.
Prescott, William (Kirk ed.)	1929	„History of the Conquest of Mexico." Edited by John Foster Kirk. George Allen & Unwin Ltd., London.
Smith, DeCost	1943	„Indian Experiences". The Caxton Printers Ltd., Caldwell, Idaho.
Taylor, Colin F.	1975	„The Warriors of the Plains". The Hamlyn Publishing Group, Ltd., London.
	1989	„Wakanyan: Symbols of Power and Ritual of the Teton Sioux". Edited by Don McCaskill. IN „Amerindian Cosmology", Cosmos 4, Yearbook of the Traditional Cosmology Society. The Canadian Journal of Native Studies, Brandon, Manitoba.
	1990	„Reading Plains Indian Artefacts: Their symbolism as cultural and historical documents". Unpublished Ph. D. Thesis. University of Essex, Dept. of Literature, Colchester, Essex.
	1993	„Saam: The Symbolic Content of Early Northern Plains Ceremonial Regalia". Bilingual Americanistik Books. Verlag für Amerikanistik, Wyk, Germany.
Taylor, Colin F.	1994	„The Plains Indians". Salamander Books Ltd. London.
Teit, James A. (Boas ed.)	1930	„The Salishan Tribes of the Western Plateaus". Edited by Franz Boas. Bureau of American Ethnology. 45th Annual Report. Smithsonian Institution. Washington D. C.
Torrence, Gaylord	1994	„The American Indian Parfleche: A Tradition of Abstract Painting". Des Moines Art Center, Des Moines.
Vestal, Stanley	1934	„Warpath: The True Story of the Fighting Sioux Told in a Biography of Chief White Bull". Houghton Mifflin, Boston.

Walker, James R. (DeMallie and Jahner eds.) 1980 „Lakota Belief and Ritual". Edited by Raymond J. DeMallie and Elaine A. Jahner. University of Nebraska Press, Lincoln and London.

West, Ian M. 1978 „Horse Sticks". IN American Indian Art magazine, Vol. 3, No. 2, Scottsdale, Arizona.

1979 „Tributes to a Horse Nation: Plains Indian Horse Effigies". IN South Dakota History, Vol. 9, No. 4, South Dakota State Historical Society, Pierre, South Dakota.

Wildschut, William (Ewers ed.) 1960 „Crow Indian Medicine Bundles". Edited by John C. Ewers. Museum of the American Indian, Heye Foundation, New York.

Wilson, Gilbert 1916 "Report of Anthropological Work on Fort Berthold Indian Reservation, to the American Museum of Natural History. Wilson Papers, Minnesota Historical Society.

Wissler, Clark 1907 „Some Protective Designs of the Dakota". American Museum of Natural History. Vol. I, Part II, New York.

1911 „Social Organization and Ritualistic Ceremonies of the Blackfoot Indians". Part I: „The Social Life of the Blackfoot Indians". American Museum of Natural History. Vol. VII, New York.

1912a „Social Organization and Ritualistic Ceremonies of the Blackfoot Indians". Part II: „Ceremonial Bundles of the Blackfoot Indians". American Museum of Natural History. Vol. VII, New York

1912b „Societies and Ceremonial Associations in the Oglala Division of the Teton-Dakota". American Museum of Natural History. Vol. XI, New York.

1913 „Societies and dance associations of the Blackfoot Indians". Anthropological Papers of The American Museum of Natural History. Vol. XI, New York.

1915 „Riding Gear of the North American Indians". Anthrop. Papers of the American Museum of Natural History. Vol. XVII. Part. I., New York.

Inhaltsverzeichnis

Acknowledgements	5
Einführung	6
Das Erscheinen des Pferdes	12
Die mystische Nation	14
Pferdebilder	16
Übernatürliche Kräfte	18
Pferde-Medizin-Kraft	22
Der Transport der Medizinpfeife und symbolische Pferdeausrüstungsgegenstände	44
Masken, Kopfschmuck und Kriegsbündel	58
Das Erbeuten von Pferden	72
Die Kräfte des Donners	78
Symbolische Bemalung	88
Abschließende Bemerkungen	98
Bibliography	100

Contents

Acknowledgements	5
Introduction	7
The coming of the horse	13
The mystical nation	15
Horse images	17
Supernatural powers	19
Horse medicine power	23
Transporting the Medicine Pipe and symbolic horse accoutrements	45
Masks, Head Ornaments and War Bundles	59
Capturing horses	73
Thunder Powers	79
Symbolic painting	89
Concluding remarks	99
Bibliography	100

Colin F. Taylor

Saam

The Symbolic Content of Early Northern Plains Ceremonial Regalia

The symbolism in the art of the Native Americans is one of the most significant and interesting scientific subjects. For example, analyses of the decoration on the costumes of a medicine pipe owner - the quillwork, fringes and paintings on his shirt and leggings - suggest that little, if any, of the embellishment was merely aesthetic. Much had a meaning associated with the supernatural powers, which dominated sky, earth and water.

Generally, it was initiates and holy men or women alone who most fully understood the symbolic content, much of which was restricted knowledge and excluded from the common man.

Many elements of this culture were lost during the reservation period, and to reconstruct the meaning of patterns and symbols is a most difficult and daunting task.

This book contains a lecture, which the British scholar **Colin F. Taylor** gave at the *PLAINS INDIAN ART SYMPOSIUM* in Cody, Wyoming, in October 1991, relating to the results of several years' research on religious and military symbolism of the Northern Plains. It is based on extensive knowledge and careful studies of records and statements of field-workers and shamans, of mythology, ritual and traditions, together with an examination of relevant artifacts in the ethnographic collections.

This important study is published in a bilingual edition *(English/German)*.
Pp. 86, 33 ill., some in color, bibliography, clothbound,
dust-jacket, size 17.5 x 24.5 cm.

ISBN 3-924696-85-3   DM 30,--

Verlag für Amerikanistik
P. O. Box 1332 - D-25931 Wyk
Phone 04681/3112 - Fax 04681/3258

Payments by **Mastercard** *or* **Visa** *welcome!*

Colin F. Taylor
WAPA'HA
The Plains Feathered Head-dress

There is hardly any part of the warrior costume of the North American Indian recognized as most typical by observers, than the flaring feathered head-dress. It still seems to be the symbol in general for the Plains Indians. Surprisingly enough, in spite of this „perpetual image", as the author of this book expresses it, there are only very few studies about this impressive regalia.

Colin F. Taylor, a worldwide well-known Plains Indian expert, has been dealing with this subject for 30 years.

In September 1993, he gave a lecture on the feathered head-dress at the PLAINS INDIAN ART SYMPOSIUM in Cody, Wyoming, in which he summarized the results of a long-time research in the relevant collections around the world, and of studies of sources and literature.

This outstanding paper on one of the most interesting elements of the material and spiritual culture of the Native Americans, annotated and enhanced by the author, is presented here in a bilingual book edition *(English/German)*. It considers the Indian styles of headgear in general as well as the symbolic content of this regalia, and touches too the feather techniques and structural elements.

From the contents: *Perpetual image, changing meaning: the Plains feathered head-dress - from Four Bears to Iron Tail - Early history: The Woodlands - The Plains - Styles of symbolic headgear - Origins of the flaring style head-dress - Distribution of the flaring style head-dress - Distribution of styles: a further and more detailed discussion - The straight-up style- The flaring bonnet - the horned bonnet - Trailer head-dresses - Feather techniques - Plains headbands - Symbolism - Bibliography*

Pp. 117, 42 ill., several in color, clothbound, dust-jacket, size 17.5 x 24.5 cm.
ISBN 3-89510-002-1   DM 35,--

Verlag für Amerikanistik
P. O. Box 1332 - D-25931 Wyk
Phone 04681/3112 - Fax 04681/3258

The German publishing house for Native American history!